A History of the Alligator

Florida's Favorite Reptile

Donald D. Spencer

Schiffer Publishing Ltd

4880 Lower Valley Road, Atglen, Pennsylvania 19310

This book is based mainly on the postcard and illustration collection of the author, a longtime student of Florida history. However, the postcard views on pages 42, 59, 67, 83, 105, 106, 111, 122, 125, 126 and 131 are from the collection of his daughter, Susan Spencer-Hayes, a fellow Alligator Postcard collector. The photo on page 62 is from the state of Florida's Archives.

The Alligator souvenirs shown on page 25 are from the collections of the author's son, Steven Spencer, and daughter, Sherrie Spencer. The souvenirs on page 141 are from the collection of his daughters, Susan and Sherrie.

Other Schiffer Books by Donald D. Spencer:
St. Johns River, An Illustrated History,
978-0-7643-2826-8, $24.99
Greetings from Jacksonville, Florida,
978-0-7643-2958-6, $24.99
Greetings from Orlando & Winter Park,
1902-1950: 978-0-7643-2966-1, $24.99

Other Schiffer Books on Related Subjects:
The Great Swamp: New Jersey's Natural Treasure,
978-0-7643-2822-0, $19.95
Fort Lauderdale Memories: A Postcard History 1900-1960,
978-0-7643-2828-2, $24.99

Designed by Stephanie Daugherty
Type set in Ballpark/Souvenir Lt BT/Humanist 521 BT
ISBN: 978-0-7643-3083-4
Printed in China

Schiffer Books are available at special discounts for bulk purchases for sales promotions or premiums. Special editions, including personalized covers, corporate imprints, and excerpts can be created in large quantities for special needs. For more information contact the publisher:

Published by Schiffer Publishing Ltd.
4880 Lower Valley Road
Atglen, PA 19310
Phone: (610) 593-1777
Fax: (610) 593-2002
E-mail: Info@schifferbooks.com

For the largest selection of fine reference books on this and related subjects, please visit our web site at: www.schifferbooks.com We are always looking for people to write books on new and related subjects. If you have an idea for a book please contact us at the above address.

This book may be purchased from the publisher. Include $5.00 for shipping. Please try your bookstore first. You may write for a free catalog.

In Europe, Schiffer books are distributed by:
Bushwood Books
6 Marksbury Ave.
Kew Gardens
Surrey TW9 4JF England
Phone: 44 (0) 20 8392-8585
Fax: 44 (0) 20 8392-9876
E-mail: info@bushwoodbooks.co.uk
Website: www.bushwoodbooks.co.uk
Free postage in the U.K., Europe;
air mail at cost.

Dedication

To my granddaughter, Selena Rae Alger,
a University of Florida Gator.

Contents

About the Postcard

It will be readily apparent from the variety of illustrations in this book that postcard publishers saw Alligators as an attractive subject to feature on their cards. In the early 1900s, when picture postcards were at the height of their popularity and millions went through the postal system daily, both photographic and artist-drawn scenes of Alligators went on sale for Florida residents and tourists to buy and send. Well-known comic artists used Alligator situations as the basis of postcard cartoons. These early twentieth century postcards are today extremely popular and widely collected. Rare examples are artist drawn cards, Real Photo postcards, Alligator hunting scenes, comic cards, and Alligator Border postcards. Postcard prices vary from $1 or $2 for common Alligator scenes to around $100 for many of the 165 cards in the Alligator Border Series.

Early Postcards

Postcards first appeared in Austria in 1869, and then England and France in 1870. These early European cards carried no images; there was only space on one side for an address, the reverse side was for a message. But they enjoyed an advantage over first-class letter mail; they could be mailed at a reduced rate of postage. The first picture postcards appeared in Germany in 1870. The United States began to issue picture postcards in 1873 in conjunction with the Columbian Exposition in Chicago. These were illustrations on government printed postal cards and on privately printed souvenir cards. On May 19, 1898 private printers were granted permission, by an act of Congress, to print and sell cards that bore the inscription "Private Mailing Card." The government granted the use of the word "POST CARD" to private printers on December 4, 1901. In this era, private citizens began to take black and white photographs and have them printed on paper with postcard backs. These cards are commonly called Real Photo Postcards.

Real Photo Postcards

It was in 1902 that Eastman Kodak marketed its postcard size photographic papers. They quickly followed with a folding camera (model No. 3A) that was specially designed for making Real Photo Postcards or RPPs. To make matters even simpler, an amateur photographer could mail the camera with exposed film to Eastman Kodak. They would develop and print the postcards and return them to the sender with a reloaded camera. These innovations in photography as applied to the postcard captured the public's imagination. It had become possible for anyone who owned a camera to make personalized photo postcards.

Postcards Become Popular

The picture postcard did not come into common use in the United States until after 1900. It was about 1902 that the postcard craze hit the country and it was not long before a wide variety of printed postcards were available: advertising, expositions, political, greetings, and more. Collectors would send postcards to total strangers in faraway places, asking for local cards in return. Some collectors specialized in railroad depots, street scenes, cemeteries, churches, courthouses, farms, holidays, animals, military scenes, casinos, ethnic images, sports, hotels, transportation devices, parks, bathing beauties, industrial scenes, beach scenes, plants, lighthouses, restaurants, space, amusement parks, rivers, Steamboats, plants, agricultural products, and even comic cards; others collected anything they could find. Postcard albums, bought by the millions, were filled with every sort of postcard ever issued. The craze was actually worldwide since many countries had postcards. Acceptance by the public was immediate and enthusiastic. Postcards afforded an easy means of communication. They were an early version of today's email, though slower, of course, relying as they did on mail service.

The Divided Back Postcards

Before March 1, 1907, it was illegal to write any message on the same side of the card as the address. For that reason early postcards often have handwriting all over the sides of the picture, and sometimes right across it. Many an otherwise beautiful card was defaced in this way. When postcards first started to go through the mail, they were postmarked at the receiving post office as well as that of the sender, making it easy to see the time involved between post offices—sometimes remarkably brief! The volume of postcards was an important reason for discontinuing the unnecessary second marking about 1910. For years postcards cost only a nickel for six and the postage was a penny, right up to World War II.

The most popular American postcards up to World War I were those made in Germany from photographs supplied by American publishers. At the time of the postcard craze, of course, color photography was still something of a rarity and not commercially viable. For the color cards, black and white photos were touched up, hand-colored, and then generally reproduced by lithography. Lithography consists of transferring the image to a lithographic stone, offset to a rubber blanket, and then printed onto paper. The details in the German produced cards were extremely sharp, and the best of them technically have never been matched since.

The German postcard industry folded in the summer of 1914, when the war struck Europe, and never revived. Postcards produced during the years 1907 and 1915 had a divided back: the address was to be written on the right side; the left side was for writing messages. Millions of postcards were published during these years. Postcard collectors have hailed these opening years of the twentieth century as the "Golden Age" of postcards. During the golden era of the picture postcard, billions of postcards rolled off the printing presses. In 1917 the United States entered World War I and the postcard craze ended.

White Border Postcards

With the advent of World War I, the supply of postcards for American consumption switched from Germany to England and the United States. Postcards printed in the United States during the years 1915 to 1930 were classified as White Border cards. To save ink, a colorless border was left around the view. These postcards were of a poorer quality as compared to the cards printed in Germany.

Linen Postcards

In 1930 the "linen" textured card was introduced and was popular until 1950. While this card was less expensive to produce, it reduced the clarity of detail in the pictures. These cheap cards are typically printed in vivid colors on paper with a crosshatched surface, which resembled linen fabric. "Linen" refers to the texture-like feel of the cardboard stock. The cards of this period romanticized the images of diners, gas stations, hotels, commercial buildings, and tourist attractions. Using the photographic image of an establishment, all undesirable features, such as background clutter, people, telephone poles, and even cars were removed by airbrushing. World War II occupied most people's attention during much of this period, but the prosperity that followed soon was reflected in cards from communities all over the United States.

Photochrome Postcards

In 1950 the "photochrome" or "chrome" postcard, with a glossy finish, replaced the linen card. This type of finish allowed for a very sharp reproduction of the picture, however, the cards seem to have lost much of the role and nature of earlier cards. The chrome card, which is offered for sale today in gift shops, is where full-color photographic images are reproduced as a half tone on modern lithography presses. A varnish or lamination is applied on the card to give it a shiny look. In 1970, a king-sized chrome card (4.125-inch by 5.875-inch) was introduced and by 1978 it was in general use everywhere. This card is also called a continental or modern postcard.

Collecting Postcards

If you have ever browsed through boxes of vintage postcards in an antique shop or at a flea market booth for quaint views of your hometown, you may well be on the way to becoming a deltiologist, which is the collecting and study of postcards. The word deltiology comes from "delti" (little picture) and "logy" (the theory, science, or study of).

Postcards are a compact collectible with a history. They are snapshots in time. During a time when the main communication was by letter, which meant the long process of writing it, the postcard was a quick, simple means of saying "hello" with a picture "worth-a-thousand-words." The Postcards' popularity became evident when, in 1908, the U.S. Post Office cited there were over 677 million postcards mailed despite the U.S. population being only about 89 million—and this doesn't include those kept as souvenirs. Today, postcard collecting has become the number one hobby in the United States.

Introduction

One of the few living relatives of the prehistoric dinosaurs, the American Alligator has become integrated into the lives of Americans like no other species. This remarkable reptile has intrigued explorers, writers, artists, scientists, residents, cartoonists, tourists, filmmakers, photographers, and others for nearly five hundred years. Before the Spanish founded Florida in 1513, the Alligator was well known to Native Americans. Many tribes developed songs or dances about the Alligator and many ate their meat. Some tribes used Alligator skins to make ceremonial drums.

The Alligator has become a symbol, mascot, pet, medicine, handbag, food, luggage, souvenir, and a popular Florida attraction. Florida's resident reptile has been researched, photographed, feared, hunted, farmed, tanned, sold, eaten, worshipped, sculpted, and displayed. It is the basis of many comic strips, books, horror stories, magazine articles, songs, postcards, newspaper columns, folklore, novels, political cartoons, paintings, sculptures, movies, drawings, and ceramics.

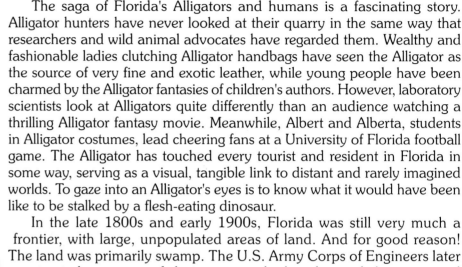

The saga of Florida's Alligators and humans is a fascinating story. Alligator hunters have never looked at their quarry in the same way that researchers and wild animal advocates have regarded them. Wealthy and fashionable ladies clutching Alligator handbags have seen the Alligator as the source of very fine and exotic leather, while young people have been charmed by the Alligator fantasies of children's authors. However, laboratory scientists look at Alligators quite differently than an audience watching a thrilling Alligator fantasy movie. Meanwhile, Albert and Alberta, students in Alligator costumes, lead cheering fans at a University of Florida football game. The Alligator has touched every tourist and resident in Florida in some way, serving as a visual, tangible link to distant and rarely imagined worlds. To gaze into an Alligator's eyes is to know what it would have been like to be stalked by a flesh-eating dinosaur.

In the late 1800s and early 1900s, Florida was still very much a frontier, with large, unpopulated areas of land. And for good reason! The land was primarily swamp. The U.S. Army Corps of Engineers later constructed a system of drainage canals that diverted the unwanted water into the ocean.

It was said back then that one of Florida's greatest resources was Northerners. They came by the hundreds on Steamships or railroad, first to Jacksonville and then to other cities further south. Large hotels were built to accommodate these travelers. Most of Florida's early visitors wanted to see Alligators; the Alligator motif adorned nearly every kind of tourist item imaginable — including the postcard.

In the early 1900s, when picture postcards were at the height of their popularity, millions went through the postal system daily. Both photographs and artist-drawn Florida Alligator scenes went on sale for locals and tourists to buy and send. Well-known comic artists used Alligator situations as the basis of postcard cartoons. The trend continued even after World War I when the picture postcard generally became less used as the telephone took over some of its functions. Thus many of the illustrations in this book are post-1918, though generally the cards of the 1920s and 1930s were of inferior quality to their pre-World War I predecessors.

This book is simply a collection of interesting Florida Alligator scenes selected from the author's collection. A bit of historical or descriptive information for many of the scenes has been provided in an attempt to add interest. The main objective has been to show some views of Florida Alligators in the early days of the twentieth century.

The Alligator

Alligators are remnants of a prehistoric era. When dinosaurs became extinct, these modern-day contemporaries of dinosaurs continued to flourish and have survived their prehistoric relatives into the twenty-first century. There are two true species, or kinds, of Alligators: American and Chinese. The American Alligator lives in Southeastern United States. They live throughout Florida and Louisiana and are found in parts of Alabama, Arkansas, Georgia, Mississippi, North Carolina, Oklahoma, South Carolina, and Texas. Alligators are found in all of Florida's sixty-seven counties. The Chinese Alligator lives in China.

Alligators have fascinated people for centuries. Many tall tales have been told about these giant reptiles with the long tails. They are the original models for many dragons, serpents, and other fairy tale monsters.

The true story of the Alligator is even more fascinating. Spanish adventurers exploring Florida gave them the name "el legarto," which means "the lizard" in Spanish. In English, the word became "aligarto," and then "Alligator." Alligators are commonly called "gators."

Alligators, along with Crocodiles, caiman, and gharials, make up a group of animals known as crocodilians, which are the world's largest reptiles. A reptile is a cold-blooded animal that has scaly skin, lays eggs, and breathes with lungs. All crocodilians live in similar places—where the water meets the land and the weather is warm. Most of them prefer to swim in freshwater. But some, like the saltwater American Crocodile, swim mostly in salt water. Most reptiles have very small brains. But crocodilians have larger brains and are probably the most intelligent reptiles of all.

The Alligator has a large, slightly rounded body, with thick limbs, a broad head, and a very powerful tail, which it uses to propel itself through water. The tail accounts for half the Alligator's length. While Alligators move very quickly in water, they are generally slow moving on land, although they can be quick for short distances.

The story of the American Alligator is one of both drastic decline and complete recovery—it is truly one of the prominent success stories of the nation's endangered species program.

Alligators Home in Florida. The reptile known as *Alligator mississippiensis* (American Alligator) has inhabited the state for about ten million years. It's one of only two living species of Alligators in the world. The other is the rare Chinese Alligator (*Alligator sinensis*) of the Yangtze River. Scientists say that time has done nothing to improve its looks. The Alligator was its same homely self when it first appeared on earth. *Circa 1908, $3-5.*

10

Native of Florida. If the Alligator seems to be a prehistoric relic—it is. Its relatives, during the age of dinosaurs, had skulls six feet long! Fossils this size have been found. One can imagine the size of the whole animal. The Alligator is a reptile and spends its life in the water or on shore. *Copyright 1908, $3-5.*

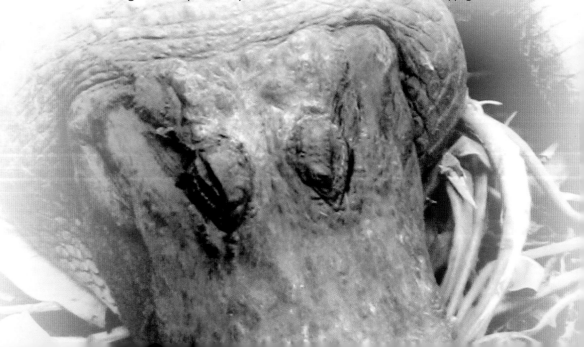

Resting Alligator. Several million Alligators live in Florida. They live in lakes, rivers, ponds, marshes, creeks, swamps, and man-made canals. Throughout history, these reptilian carnivores have been hunted, worshipped, feared, and tamed. Among Native Americans, many tribes developed songs or dances about the Alligator and ate their meat. Some tribes used Alligator skins to make ceremonial drums. The Alligator serves as a visual, tangible link to distant and rarely imagined worlds. To gaze into an Alligator's eyes is to know what it would have been like to be stalked by flesh-eating dinosaur. *Circa 1970s, $1-3.*

16ᵗʰ Century Alligator Hunt

The first European artist to visit Florida, or the New World, was a Frenchman named Jacques LeMoyne, who arrived on the banks of the St. Johns River in 1564. His are the first pictures we have of Florida Indians. However, they were drawn after LeMoyne returned to Europe, and his memory undoubtedly exaggerated the size of the Alligators he had seen.

LeMoyne also described the way the Indians attacked Alligators:

"They put up, near a river, a little hut full of cracks and holes, and in this station a watchman, so that he can see the Alligators, and hear them, a good way off; for, when driven by hunger, they come out of the rivers, and crawl about on the islands after prey, and, if they find none, they make a frightful noise that can be heard for half a mile. Then the watchman calls the rest of the watch, who are in readiness; and, taking a portion, ten or twelve feet long, of the stem of a tree, they go out to find the reptile, who is crawling along with his mouth wide open, all ready to catch one of them if he can; and with the greatest quickness they push the pole, small end first, as deep as possible down his throat, so that the roughness and irregularity of the bark may hold it from being got out again. Then they turn the Alligator over on his back, and with clubs and arrows pound and pierce his belly, which is softer; for his back, especially if he is an old one, is impenetrable, being protected by hard scales. This is the Indians way of hunting Alligators; by which they are, nevertheless, so much annoyed that they have to keep up a regular watch against them both day and night, as we should do against the most dangerous enemy."

The Captured Gator. This drawing was done from firsthand observation by French artist Jacques LeMoyne, who visited Florida in 1564. It shows Timucua Indians forcing a long pole down an Alligator's throat so that it can be flipped over, exposing its soft underbelly, to attack. In the background Indians are killing an overturned Alligator with weapons. *From an engraving by Flemish engraver Theodore DeBry of the LeMoyne painting. Circa 1591, $5-7.*

William Bartram's Battling Alligators

On March 31, 1773, the great naturalist, William Bartram, embarked on a journey of discovery that took him through seven modern states and over 2,500 miles. He published an account of his journatl in 1791 in *Travels*. He became the greatest authority on the natural sciences during the earliest years of American history. No author had *ever* written about nature and science from such a personal standpoint as Bartram did. He traveled through a region that was still a wilderness, much of it uninhabited and still in its natural state. He wrote of an account of battling Alligators on the St. Johns River:

Behold him rushing forth from the flags and reeds. His enormous body wells. His plaited tail brandished high, floats upon the lake. The waters like a cataract descend from his opening jaws. Clouds of smoke issue from his dilated nostrils. The earth trembles with his thunder. When immediately from the opposite coast of the lagoon, emerges from the deep his rival companion. They suddenly dart upon each other. The boiling surface of the tlake marks their rapid course, and a terrific conflict commences. They now sink to the bottom folded together in horrid wreaths. The water becomes thick and discoloured. Again they rise, their jaws clap together, re-echoing through the deep surrounding forests. Again they sink, when the contest ends at the muddy bottom of the lake, and the vanquished makes a hazardous escape, hiding himself in the muddy turbulent waters and sedge on a distant shore. The proud victor, exulting, returns to the place of action. The shores and forests resound his dreadful roar, together with the triumphing shouts of the plaited tribes around, witnesses of the horrid combat.

Bartram was criticized by some people for his vivid description of the battling Alligators; many who had never seen an Alligator doubted him, believing the story to be embellished.

A 19th Century Hunter Describes the Gator

Old Floridians often tell strange stories of the Alligator's strength, fleetness, and strategy. In 1874, an Alligator hunter in Jacksonville gave a brief description of these characteristics.

The 'gaiter, sir, is ez quick ez lightnin', and ez nasty. He kin out swim a deer, and he hez dun it, too; he swims mor'n two-thirds out o' the water, and when he ketches you, sir, he jest wabbles you right over 'n over, a hundred times, or mo', sir, ez quick ez the wind; and you're dead in no time, sir. When a dog sees one he allus begins to yelp, sir, for a 'gaiter is mighty fond of a dog... Nobody can't tell how old them old fellows is, sir; I reckon nigh on to a hundred years, them biggest ones. Thar's some old devils in them lagoons you see off the St. Johns River; they lie thar very quiet, but it would be a good tussle if one of you was out thar in a small boat, sir. They won't always fight; sometimes they run away very meek/ the best way to kill 'em is to put a ball in the eye, sir; thar's no use in wasting shot on a 'gaiter's hide. When the boys wants sport, sir, they git a long green pole, and sharpen it; 'n then they find a 'gaiter's hole in the marsh, and put the pole down it, then the 'gaiter he snaps at it, 'n hangs on to it, 'n the boys get together, 'n pull him out, 'n put a rope around' his neck, and set him to fighin' with another 'gaiter. O Lord! Reckon 't would make yo' har curl to see the tails fly.

Attacking A Female Gator

The following description of a Steamboat trip on the Ocklawaha River is from the 1875 *Guide to Florida* by Edward G. Jenkins.

But the prominent living object to the stranger in these out-of-the way places is the Alligator, whose paradise is in the swamps of Florida. Here he finds a climate that almost the year round suits his delicate constitution; and, while his kindred in the Louisiana swamps find it necessary to retire into the mud to escape the cold of winter, the Florida representative of the tribe is happy in the enjoyment of the upper world the year round. It was a comical and a provoking sight to see these creatures, when indisposed to get out of our way, turn up their piggish eyes in speculative mood at the sudden interruption of a rifle-ball against their mailed sides, but all the while seemingly unconscious that any harm against their persons was intended. Like Achilles, however, they possess a vulnerable point, which is just in front of the spot where the huge head works upon the spinal column. There is, of necessity, at this place a joint in the armor, and a successful hunter, after much experience, seldom lets one of the reptiles escape. If any philanthropist has ever objected to the slaughter, the circumstance is not remembered in the swamps and everglades of Florida. On one occasion we fired into a herd of Alligators, and the noise of two or three shots caused all but one to finally disappear. For some reason it seemed difficult to get the remaining one to move, the creature lying with its head exposed to our gaze, looking as demoniac as possible. A bullet, which struck somewhere in the vicinity of its jaws, touched its feelings, and then, with a grunt not unlike that of a hog, it buried itself in the muddy water. This unwillingness to move was then explained by the appearance of a large number of young Alligators, which, in the confusion came to the surface like so many chips. We had, without being aware of it, attacked the mother while she was protecting her nest.

Fighting Alligators. Botanist William Bartram traveled to the Florida wilderness in 1774 and wrote about what he saw. He made this sketch of fighting Alligators in the St. Johns River near Jacksonville. The account of his journey of discovery was published in 1791 as *Travels*. It was a new kind of nature writing that combined scientific observation with lyrical descriptions of the natural world, including the humans and animals that inhabited it. *Circa 1791, $5-7.*

A Steamboat Trip Up St. Johns River

In the late 1800s, a Steamboat trip up the St. Johns and Ocklawaha Rivers, reaching almost the center of the Florida peninsula, became a favorite excursion for American tourists wealthy enough to afford it. The trip began at Jacksonville, with the Steamboats often stopping at Palatka for the night. A stern-powered Steamboat was then taken to Silver Springs, via the Ocklawaha River. A favorite sport on those journeys was shooting at Alligators basking along the banks of the two rivers as the boat passed by.

An 1800s Alligator Skinning

Most of the Alligators killed in the winter by Northern "sportsmen" were shot while they were sunning themselves on a bank or beach, after a long sleep in the muddy bottoms of lakes or rivers, or while migrating from one body of water to another. The novices who killed large Alligators at such times generally liked to have themselves and their victims photographed, so they were able to furnish ocular proof to their Northern friends that they actually destroyed a "Florida dragon." These gentlemen also seemed anxious to get a lady or two in the group, and no picture was thought complete without the usual African American butcher engaged in flaying the carcass. Friends of the gentlemen who killed the saurians no doubt looked upon them as the most daring of heroes, yet if the facts concerning some of these victorious scenes were told they would bring the Nimrods less praise than ridicule.

One of these ridiculous photographs depicted a man, in full sporting toggery, sitting on a campstool, with a rifle across his knees, in front of a huge Alligator, which an African American was carefully dissecting. A large tent occupied the background, and groups of palmettos were visible on the right and left. The picture looked innocent and real enough, yet the accessories were grouped for the occasion, and all the principal figure in the scene had to do with the Alligator was to help tow it to where it was photographed after the African American had killed it with an axe while it was enjoying its noon siesta.

The previous remarks were not intended to imply that the majority of sportsmen do not kill the reptiles in a thoroughly sportsman-like manner, but rather to explain how so many photographs of Florida scenes make the skinning of Alligators seem so common.

An Old Alligator Hunter

In 1885, two men tied their rowboat to the stern of the Steamboat *Volusia*, which was operating on St. Johns River. One of the men tossed a dozen Alligator hides up on the deck. He wore a pair of dirty pantaloons, a butternut colored woolen shirt, an old-fashioned coat, and a black slouched hat. The six foot tall suntanned man carried a double-barreled rifle. He was a gator hunter.

The hunter was in the habit of boarding the *Volusia* and going up on the Steamboats' Captain's deck where he watched the passengers, who invariably spent the day shooting at Alligators that were sunning themselves in the marshy places surrounding the lakes and lagoons. If a passenger killed an Alligator, the spot was marked. Occasionally three or four Alligators would be killed inside of three miles. The hunter would then cast off in his small boat, retrace his course, and skin the animals. He got seventy-five cents for each hide delivered in Jacksonville. At this time he was filling an order from a London firm, through a Jacksonville merchant, for 3,000 hides.

Collecting Alligator Teeth

During the winter months in the late 1880s, crowds of Northern men flocked to Enterprise, a community on the St. Johns River. Many of them employed their time by hunting Alligators. The guests sat upon the verandah of the hotel hour after hour polishing Alligator teeth with sandpaper and buckskin. Every day somebody brought an Alligator that had been shot in the vicinity. After killing the Alligator, it was hitched to the stern of the Steamboat with a chain and towed to the beach in front of the hotel. An African American was hired to cut off the Alligator's head and skin him. After the head was cut off, it was buried for two weeks. This was necessary to secure the reptile's teeth. Alligator teeth sold from two dollars a piece up to five dollars. Some African Americans made a living by carving flowers and curious figures on the teeth.

On the Ocklawaha River, Fla.

On the Ocklawaha River. In the mid-1800s, swamp sounds along the Ocklawaha River were drowned out by the earliest Steamboats to ply those waters. This view shows the *Astatula* steamer cautiously pointing her way through the dense foliage on the Ocklawaha River. The diverse landscape of the Ocklawaha River area provides habitat and feeding areas for a wide variety of wildlife species, including Alligators and exotic birds. Steamboat passengers enjoyed watching the birds among the flowering vines, Alligators lazing sleepily along the banks, and the occasional glimpse of a panther, deer, or bear. *Circa 1904, $18-20.*

Hunting Alligators

Before laws were put into place to protect the Alligator, it was severely depleted throughout Florida. Luckily, Alligators also occupied millions of acres of swamps and wetlands that were impenetrable by hunters. Following the enactment of effective measures by federal and state governments, Alligator populations rapidly increased and the animals moved back to replenish the depleted areas.

Today, hunting is allowed, but is carefully regulated. Several thousand tags are sold each year. The hunter pays a fee for each tag, which allows him to kill one Alligator. The number of Alligators that can be taken from an area depends on the population density of the animals there. Regulated hunting doesn't stop the Alligator population from growing.

This act, combined with the reduced demand for Alligator skins resulting from a decline in many traditional retail markets, virtually eliminated poaching. Although much has been said about the poaching of Florida Alligators during the 1960s, Alligators remained abundant in remote and inaccessible areas. The rapid recovery of the reptiles throughout the 1970s, once they were effectively protected, suggests they endured poaching better than once thought.

In 1974, the Florida Game and Fresh Water Fish Commission began conducting surveys to document annual population trends of the Alligator. Results show a progressive increase from 1974 to the present.

Alligator Populations —
Past and Present

By the 1940s, Florida's Alligator population had noticeably decreased. Imposition of hunting restrictions in the 1940s and 1950s slowed the decline, but illegal poaching during the late 1950s and 1960s resulted in a further decrease in most Florida Alligator populations.

Despite the complete protection of Alligators under a 1962 Florida law, extensive Alligator poaching continued until 1970. At that time, an amendment to the federal Lacey Act made the interstate shipment of illegally taken Alligators a federal violation.

Alligator Hunting. Shooting Alligators made a serious dent in the population of these reptiles and later aroused the ire of such pioneer conservationists as Harriet Beecher Stowe. By 1890, shooting wildlife from boats was prohibited. *Circa 1850, $3-5.*

Alligator Habitats in Florida

Alligators live in all Florida counties, but are most common in the major river drainage basins and large lakes in the central and southern portions of the state. They also can be found in marshes, swamps, ponds, drainage canals, and phosphate-mine settling ponds and ditches. Alligators are tolerant of poor water quality and occasionally inhabit brackish marshes along the coast. A few even venture into salt water.

Mature Alligators seek open water areas during the April-to-May courtship and breeding season. After mating, the females move into marsh areas to nest in June and early July, remaining there until the following spring. Males generally prefer open and deeper waters year found. Alligators less than four feet long typically inhabit the marshy areas of lakes and rivers. Dense vegetation in these habitats provides protective cover and many of the preferred foods of young Alligators.

"Glad to Meet You" in Florida—F188. Alligators are part of the "real" Florida and may be found wherever there is a natural body of water. They are among the oldest, largest, and most advanced reptiles on earth. Residents and visitors alike must realize that Alligators are an important part of Florida's heritage, and that these prehistoric reptiles play an important role in the ecology of Florida's wetlands. An understanding of these facts and broader knowledge of Alligator habits will ensure that humans and Alligators continue their long-term coexistence. Remember that Alligators were here long before us and have proven to be remarkably adaptable. *Cancelled 1943, $3-5.*

Alligator Reproduction

Sexual maturity is dependent on the size of the Alligator, and both sexes first reach sexual maturity when they are about six feet long. In the wild, this takes about ten to twelve years; however, in captivity, under ideal conditions, Alligators can reach sexual maturity much sooner.

Like most animals that live in temperate climates, Alligators breed in the spring. The Bull Alligators announces its presence by loud bellowing. Choruses of bellowing, breeding males and females can be heard across the wetlands during the spring breeding season, which is from March to June. Alligators also communicate acoustically. The best-known performance in this repertoire is the head slap. An animal will lift its head above the water, with bottom jaw just visible, and hold that position for a period of time. Then, without warning, it quickly opens its jaws and slams them shut an instant before it smacks them on the surface of the water. The head slaps and bellowing establish and maintain long-term social relationships.

Sometime in June female Alligators begin to build nests. The cone-shaped nest is a mound made from mud and vegetation that are present at the next site. After building the nest, the female digs out a vase-shaped hole in the top and deposits from twenty to seventy eggs. Then she covers the eggs with a layer of vegetation. The female Alligator guards her nest from intruders. She will attack lizards, skunks, raccoons, storks, pigs, opossums, wild boars, and bears that come to make a meal of her eggs. She may also threaten humans who get too close to her nest.

As young Alligators get ready to hatch in mid-August through mid-September, they begin to make high-pitched, grunting sounds. The females respond to these calls by using their mouths and forefeet to remove the nesting material covering the young, thus liberating the six- to eight-inch hatchlings from the nest.

Hatchlings remain in groups called "pods" through their first winter and may stay in the vicinity of the nest for two to three years. Female Alligators may defend their young until the next summer.

The first two years are the most critical in the life of an Alligator. Eighty percent or more may fall victim to wading birds, raccoons, bobcats, otters, snakes, large bass, and even larger Alligators. Once an Alligator exceeds four feet, it is relatively safe from predators, but still may be vulnerable to cannibalism.

Feeding Habits

Alligators are carnivores. Young Alligators eat insects, snails and other invertebrates, frogs and small fish. At a length of about six feet they begin to feed predominantly on fish, turtles, snakes, water birds, and small mammals. Larger Alligators occasionally take deer, wild boars, and domestic calves.

Alligators will readily eat carrion, and, in fact, may prefer it to fresh meat. They are basically opportunistic feeders and will eat almost anything, including such objects as sticks, stones, fishing lures, and aluminum cans.

Other Alligator Behavioral Activities

Although Alligators don't hibernate in the true sense, they do undergo periods of dormancy in cold weather. It's common for an Alligator to excavate a cave in the bank of a waterway and enlarge the inner chamber so a portion is above water level. Alligators in north Florida are inactive during the coldest winter months. Throughout the rest of the state they generally remain active year round.

Females usually have small territories while males can occupy ranges greater than two square miles. Researchers in Louisiana tracked one adult male for thirty-three miles through the marshes. Individuals of both sexes are most likely to become more active and extend their ranges during the April-to-May courtship and breeding season.

Young Alligators stay in the area where they were hatched until they are approximately two to three years old. They then begin to disperse in search of food, perhaps driven away by larger Alligators. Periods of drought also can cause Alligators to relocate if their water holes dry up.

Alligators in Nest, Florida

A new Alligator is born. Just minutes from the egg and looking like real baby dragons, these eight-inch black and yellow striped hatchlings will start life fending for themselves. With needle-sharp teeth and the ability to swim and catch small fish, frogs, and insects, they will grow almost a foot in length each year. Ironically, eighty percent of baby Alligators don't survive, falling victim to wading birds, snakes, raccoons, and even large bass. *Copyright 1907, $3-5.*

Alligator's Nest. Alligators build their nests above the ground out of leaves, branches, and mud. After these materials have been gathered, the mother Alligator shapes them into a mound about six feet wide and three feet high. She scoops out a hole in the center of the mound and lays twenty to seventy eggs in it. Then she covers it over. As the leaves and branches rot, they give off enough heat to keep the eggs warm. It takes the eggs approximately seventy-five days to hatch. Mother Alligators usually stay near their nests to guard them. If any intruder comes close, the mother will drive them away. The males will guard the nest in the female's absence. This view shows an Alligator guarding her nest. *Circa 1930s, $3-5.*

Living with Alligators

A Florida Man Eater near Miami, Fla.

1892.5

Alligators and humans have shared the marshes, swamps, and lakes of Southeastern United States for many centuries. Native Indians and early European pioneers occasionally used this reptile for food, but not until fashion markets began producing Alligator skin products did this prehistoric reptile become heavily hunted. A century of unrestricted and unregulated hunting depleted most accessible populations. Even after the passage of state regulations governing the harvest of Alligators during the 1940s, Alligator populations continued to decline due to extensive poaching. It was not until 1970, when federal laws prohibited the interstate shipment of Alligators, that these reptiles were afforded effective protection. The federal Endangered Species Act of 1973 provided further support.

Shortly after their protection began, Alligators rapidly repopulated areas once heavily hunted. Surveys established by the Game and Fresh Water Fish Commission indicated progressive increases from 1974 to 1985. During that same period Florida experienced tremendous human population growth. That trend continues today, with approximately 1,000 people moving to Florida daily. Many of these new residents seek homes on waterfront property, resulting in increased interactions between humans and Alligators.

Under no circumstances should one get close to an Alligator. They are quite agile, even on land. As with any wild animal, Alligators merit a measure of respect.

Alligators were here long before humans and have proven remarkably adaptable. Many conflicts between Alligators and people are perhaps perceived rather than real. Good judgment can reduce serious incidents to a minimum.

A Florida Man Eaten Near Miami. Do not insult an Alligator until after you have crossed the river. Large Alligators are hard to handle in the water. This postcard produces an excellent view of the inside of this reptile's mouth. The Alligator's teeth, in spite of their fierce appearance, are not used for chewing, but rather to seize and tear its food prior to swallowing it whole. Aided by a stomach that secretes gastric juices powerful enough to dissolve bones, hair, and shells, the Alligator has few digestive problems. *Cancelled 1925, $3-5.*

295   WAITING FOR A BITE IN FLORIDA

Waiting For A Bite in Florida. I don't think this young fisherman was looking for the "bite" that this postcard suggests. *Circa 1930s, $5-7.*

How Alligators Help Birds

Alligators are important in the conservation of bird life in addition to the food and drink provided by their gator holes. Alligators will gobble down any wading bird or chick they are able to catch; however, they save far more birds than they destroy. Where there are Alligators, there may also be large rookeries of nesting water birds. These are frequently located in swampy areas where the egrets, herons and ibis nest by the thousands. Raccoons, snakes, bobcats, and rats gather around, hoping to feast on the eggs and on the young birds. Beneath a rookery, the Alligators will feed chiefly on these prowling animals. And so, without intending to, they save the lives of countless birds.

Slaughtering Alligators for Hides

At the turn of the twentieth century Alligators were still being slaughtered mercilessly for their hides. Beginning in the 1870s and lasting into the mid-1960s, millions of Alligators were killed for the manufacture of handbags, attaché cases, shoes, and tourist souvenirs. As one writer put it, the Alligator was an "unlovely reptile representing dollar signs." Often the Alligator scenes were almost cute; representing the antics of a dog or cat playing with its owner.

Shared Habitat. The Alligator will, of course, eat the Great Blue Heron in the water if it gets a chance, but actually Alligators are important in the conservation of bird life. *Circa 1970s, $1-3.*

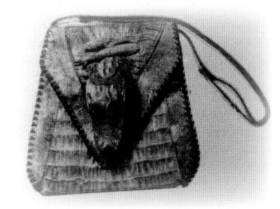

Feeding Alligators

Some people actively encourage Alligators and may try to feed them scraps of food. This is a dangerous practice, because the reptiles soon lose their normal sense of fear and then may even start to pursue people in search of food. As a result, the feeding of Alligators in Florida has been outlawed, as, of course, is either killing or disturbing the creatures.

Capturing Wild Alligators

Capturing a wild Alligator weighing a half-ton is no job for amateurs. There are many different ways to catch Alligators. Lassoing with a lariat is one way. Snag hooks, harpoons, and bait books suspended over water are other methods. When an Alligator is in a cave, a long pole with a large iron hook at the end may be used to vigorously prod the Alligator. He will then usually seize it with his mouth, and can be pulled out alive. Locating Alligators at night with a bright light is often done as the eyes of the Alligator reflect a brilliant red when hit with the light. This is called "fire-hunting."

In October 1997, an Alligator measuring fourteen feet long and weighing more than eight hundred pounds was pulled from Lake Monroe and killed as a nuisance Alligator. A trapper was called after a homeowner reported the Alligator was cruising the area, probably looking for a meal. The hunters baited the Alligator early in the morning, catching him on a large hook. The line was secured to a dock and the Alligator was allowed to thrash around until he wore himself out. After about four hours the hunters slipped a noose around the Alligator's mouth, taped it shut, and then killed him.

The Florida Game and Freshwater Fish Commission receives thousands of "nuisance" Alligator complaints from state residents. Any Alligator more the four feet in length that appears to have lost its natural fear of humans, or poses a threat to people or property, falls into the nuisance category. Five regional offices of the Game and Freshwater Fish Commission handle all Alligator complaints. Because Alligators are classified as a threatened species, they are protected under state and federal laws. Only representatives of the Commission are empowered to handle nuisance Alligators. Around forty "Nuisance Alligator" control trappers work under contract for the Commission. About 18,000 nuisance gators are reported to the state each year and licensed trappers harvest more than 10,000 of these.

FEEDING A TAME (?) ALLIGATOR. MIAMI, FLA.

Feeding A Tame (?) Alligator.
It's a dangerous practice to feed Alligators, as they don't know a hand from a handout. In Florida it's against the law to feed Alligators. *Circa 1920s, $5-7.*

At The Alligator Farm.

Alligator Farming

Alligator farming is a thriving business in Florida, with thirty or more Alligator farms in the state. This multimillion-dollar industry generates around 500,000 pounds of meat and more than 50,000 skins a year. While skin prices vary from year to year, the average price is around twenty-five dollars per foot.

Long before the fashion industry took a fancy to Alligator skins, gator meat was very popular in regions with large crocodilian populations. The hunting of Alligators for their skins so depleted the population that broad marketing of the meat was not possible. Now, with a growing network of farms and ranches raising Alligators, the populations have been replenished and this meat is available worldwide.

Alligator meat is low in calories and fat. A 100-gram piece of Alligator meat contains twenty-nine percent of the recommended daily allowance for protein, only three percent fat, sixty-five milligrams of cholesterol, and a scant 140 calories. The meat is typically sold to restaurants and wholesalers for about $5 to $7 per pound.

Lots of Gators! Before the establishment of Alligator Farms in Florida, the Alligator was in danger of becoming extinct, for the skin of the animal became highly prized as material for merchandise such as shoes and handbags. Now the farms are completely equipped for the breeding and care of Alligators, and it's a profitable business. *Cancelled 1912, $3-5.*

Alligator Wrestling

In Florida, there are a number of roadside attractions in which men wrestle with live Alligators operated by Seminole and Miccosukee Indians. In some, the handler goes into a pen and wrestles the Alligator on land. In others, a diver wrestles the Alligator underwater. Alligator wrestling is chiefly a stunt, but it does require skill and strength. A slip might mean the loss of several fingers or a hand. The Alligators used in these shows probably have been wrestled many times before. They know how the act is going to come out, and all they want is to get it over with and go back to sleep.

Alligator Wrestling.
Although it looks dangerous, this Seminole Indian wrestler is able to keep the Alligator's mouth closed with virtually no effort. The musculature for opening the jaws is extremely weak in Alligators, whereas they can shut their jaws with devastating force. Alligator wrestling is chiefly a stunt, put on for the benefit of tourists. *Circa 1950s, $1-3.*

Alligator Souvenirs

Florida wildlife has always been exotic enough for tourists to want to describe to the folks back home. Baby Alligators, alive or stuffed, became popular souvenirs of the 1940s, 1950s, and 1960s and many visitors to Florida took them home. Some Alligators souvenirs are ashtrays, bowls, plates, cups, glasses, ceramic figurines, banks, salt and pepper shakers, plastic models, toys, Alligator skin articles, oil paintings, photographs, postcards, pennants, and books.

Gator souvenirs. Gator Crossing Sign *($15-17)*; University of Florida Gator License Plate *($3-5)*; and University of Florida Pennant *($8-10)*.

Alligator Hand Bags—Casper's Genuine Alligator Products, Casper's Ostrich and Alligator Farm St. Augustine, Fla.

Original Gator Products. The Alligator has been used to produce every kind of tourist item imaginable. They have been stuffed and skinned, turned into handbags, fashionable shoes, and belts, their claws used as purses, their teeth as jewelry, and their eggs as curios. This view shows some Alligator products that were sold at Casper's Ostrich and Alligator Farm in St. Augustine. *Circa 1951, $1-3.*

Gator Attacks

As hungry Alligators search for food and mates, they often make their presence known in housing developments and commercial businesses that were built over what used to be their home turf. Peak Alligator activity starts in late March and continues through June. During that time, gator-human interaction often increases. In residential areas where there are ponds, canals, or lakes, Alligators pop up in the oddest of places... in front of garage doors, in swimming pools, in back yards, or beside busy roadways.

Although most Floridians have learned to coexist with Alligators, the potential for conflict always exists. Because of their predatory nature and large size, Alligators can, and occasionally do, attack pets. Regretfully, humans, too, occasionally are attack victims and, in rare instances, killed by large Alligators. As the state became a more popular retirement and holiday area, the situation became more serious. Also the increased demand for waterfront properties inevitably led to greater conflict with Alligators. The number of these reptiles also increased considerably as they have been protected since the early 1970s. As a result the number of attacks by Alligators on people rose and, in several cases, people were killed. Between 1948 and 2005, 351 Alligator attacks on humans were documented with several of those resulting in fatalities. Although this number of attacks may seem high, they constitute a very small percentage of water-related incidents compared to those involving water skiing, scuba diving, and boating mishaps.

Florida Boot Jack. This view, published by M. Marschall in 1903, shows a large Alligator attacking a man. This was undoubtedly a staged situation. *Cancelled 1911, $3-5.*

Documented Alligator Attacks

1948: An Alligator attacked a woman as she was swimming in a lake near the Florida Gulf Coast. The Alligator grabbed her and bit her on the arm. When the gator let up in its attack, the woman broke away and swam to shore. Two men captured the reptile, and then killed him.

• A man was snorkeling in shallow water in Juniper Springs in central Florida. Without warning, his head ended up in the jaws of a hungry eleven-foot Alligator. The gator shook him like a rag doll, held him underwater for about thirty seconds, and then released him.

1949: A woman was swimming in the Weeki Wachee River on Florida's West Coast when she was suddenly attacked by a large Alligator. The reptile seized her right arm, lost his hold, bit her left hand after flipping her over his back, and then dove out of sight. The woman recovered after twenty-three stitches were taken in her arm.

1952: An Alligator grabbed a nine-year-old girl who was fishing in a rock pit near Coral Gables. As the gator dragged her toward deep water, a ten-year old boy, fishing nearby, rushed to help. He beat the Alligator's head until it released the girl, and pulled her to safety. Later, President Harry Truman gave the boy a well-deserved award for his heroism.

July 25, 1961: Two boys were swimming with their dog in a Miami Springs canal. Suddenly an eight-foot Alligator emerged from the depths of the water and snatched the dog. When the boys called for help, a police officer ran to the bank of the canal and shot the gator. The reptile lost its hold on the dog, rolled over, and died. The dog's body floated to the surface a little later.

1969: A farmer was plowing with a tractor in the Ocala National Forest in Central Florida. As he passed the edge of a marsh, a nine-foot male gator, head lifted, jaws open, charged with amazing speed straight at the tractor. The gator clamped its teeth on the rear of the tractor, and held on. Eventually the Alligator let go of the tractor and chased the farmer into his house. The farmer called Ross Allen at the Reptile Institute at Silver Springs; Allen captured the gator and put him on display at his Alligator attraction.

1972: As a sixteen-year old girl stood cooling off in one of Florida's picturesque lakes, an eleven-foot Alligator silently stalked her. Gliding like a reptilian torpedo the final forty yards underwater, the gator attacked and killed her. It turned out that people also had routinely fed this Alligator.

THE HUNTER HUNTED, CAUGHT BY AN ALLIGATOR IN THE EVERGLADES, FLORIDA.

The Hunter Hunted.
Caught by an Alligator—an uncomfortable position to be in. *Circa 1940s, $2-4.*

1973: A sixteen-year-old girl was swimming with her father in a lake near Sarasota. Everyone who swam in this State Park knew about the Alligator that lived in the lake, so the pair ignored the reptile. Without warning, the eleven-foot, three-inch male Alligator seized the girl and drowned her. Her mangled body was found on the shore of the lake.

1975: A twelve-foot Alligator mauled a wildlife biologist in the Ocklawaha River.

September 1977: A man was swimming in Peace River in Charlotte County. However, the swimmer had company. A seven-foot female Alligator suddenly appeared out of nowhere and fatally wounded him. He was not eaten; experts concluded that the attack might have been a case of mistaken identity.

1978: A fourteen-year-old boy decided to swim across the Hidden River Canal in Martin County. He never made it to the other side. He was intercepted – and killed – by an eleven-foot male Alligator.

1984: A twelve-foot, four-inch Alligator decided that an eleven-year-old boy would make an easy-to-catch supper as the youngster was swimming in a canal in St. Lucie County. The boy was eaten alive. Children are easier to kill than adults. Unlike adults, they are less likely to fight back, and even if they do, resistance is usually short-lived and futile.

1987: A Florida State University student was snorkeling in the Wakulla Springs State Park near Tallahassee. The student foolishly left the well-posted restricted swimming area and started to lazily float down the Wakulla River. He paid the ultimate price for his mistake. He found himself face-to-face with an eleven-foot male Alligator that killed him.

• A man water skiing on a lake near Daytona Beach had his ankle seized by an eight-foot gator.

Showdown! Big George, fourteen feet, seven inches of Alligator, charges his keeper, Ross Allen, at the Reptile Institute at Silver Springs. The Alligator, no longer living, was thought to be the largest specimen in captivity. Mrs. Allen, a capable photographer, took the photo for this postcard. Allen deliberately invaded the Alligator's home territory to study its defense reaction. This postcard view is genuine, untouched, and unfaked. Big George is not kidding! Years of experience taught Allen exactly how close he could get to a charging Alligator. *Circa 1940s, $6-8.*

1988: Near the Myakka River in Charlotte County, a hungry 350-pound bull Alligator grabbed a 31-pound, four-year-old girl by her midsection. The Alligator bit her a second time and then dropped her. The gator grabbed her again and later started to feed on its prey. Officers shot the Alligator and found the girl's left leg and foot in the gator's stomach.

1996: Six-Mile Creek, which flows into St. Johns River, was the site of an Alligator attack, when a fifteen-foot gator, nicknamed Old Tail Light because of the size of his eyes, lunged at a fiberglass boat carrying a minister out for a fishing trip. The gator was protecting the carcass of a dead dog he was eating. The minister could have been the gator's next meal.

September 1997· An eleven-foot, eight-inch long, 450-pound bull Alligator attacked a swimmer in the waters of Juniper Run, about a mile upstream from Juniper Springs. The man, who had been canoeing but was swimming in the early evening, swam too close to the gator, which attacked the man, held the man's head in his powerful jaws, and shook him a few times before letting him go.

• Also in 1997 officials closed Juniper Springs after an Alligator attacked a man who was snorkeling. The Alligator bit him on the neck.

• The mutilated a body of a three-year-old boy was found near Lake Ashby, west of New Smyrna Beach. A trapper later killed an eleven-foot Alligator suspected of the attack.

April 1999: An eleven-foot bull Alligator snatched an eighty-five-pound golden retriever from a lakeside in St. Petersburg, dragging the pet under water while its owner watched in horror.

May 2001: The gnawed body of a seventy-year-old man was discovered in a Venice retention pond while an eight-foot Alligator circled it protectively. After the animal was killed, an autopsy revealed some of the man's remains in its stomach.

June 2001: One moment, a lady was treading water in Big Moss Lake. The next, she was fighting for her life as a nine-foot, six-inch Alligator clamped its powerful jaws on her left foot and began to pull her under water. Her husband, who also was in the lake, struggled to pull her free. The 350-pound gator finally let her go, but her foot was left hanging by a few shreds of flesh.

• Also in June 2001, a two-year-old child was dragged into a Polk County lake and drowned by a six-foot, six-inch Alligator that weighed five times more than the thirty-two-pound toddler. Human hair was later found in the Alligator's mouth.

• Also in 2001, while walking on a trail in the J. N. Ding Darling National Wildlife Refuge on Sanibel Island, an elderly man was attacked and killed by an Alligator.

• A seventy-year-old man in Venice was pulled into a pond by an eight-foot Alligator that mangled his head, arms, and chest, resulting in his death from bleeding. Another 2001 attack occurred near Ft. Meyers as

a man walked his dog. The Alligator bit off the man's leg form the knee down and he bled to death.

• In Everglades National Park in Southern Florida, a family was forced to jump onto a picnic table when a bold gator decided he wanted to join their party.

April 2004: A nine-foot, seven-inch long Alligator attacked a Sanibel Island lady as she gardened near a canal bank behind her home. The gator attempted to drag her into the water. The lady and her husband were able to fight the animal off.

• A woman lost her hand to an Alligator while scrubbing a pot in a lake where she routinely fed the reptiles. This incident illustrates that gators don't know a hand from a handout and shouldn't be fed.

July 2004: A lady landscaper was trimming vegetation beside a pond on Sanibel Island near Fort Myers. Suddenly, an Alligator darted out of the water and grabbed her right arm. Four men struggled for five desperate minutes to pull the lady out of the water. Finally, the reptile reluctantly released her. The animal disappeared, then resurfaced twenty-feet away, opened his mouth, and started swimming toward the lady and the rescue party, three of which were police officers. The police officers shot the Alligator in the head, killing it instantly. Six strong men were needed to lift and drag the 457-pound reptile up on the shore. The lady landscaper died two days later as a result of infections caused by the gator bites.

2005: Near Miami, researchers made the gruesome discovery of the carcass of a 13-foot Burmese python. Apparently the python had died while trying to swallow a six-foot Alligator. They speculated that as the Alligator was being partially digested, it tried to claw at the python's stomach.

2006: At Lake Parker, near Lakeland, police found a man clenched in an Alligator's jaw in chest-deep water. It took four officers twenty minutes of tug-of-war with the gator before they managed to rescue the man. Later, an 11-foot, 9-inch, 600-pound Alligator, thought to be the attacking gator, was trapped and killed.

• A 10-foot Alligator in Fort Myers snapped at a bobbing volleyball while residents of an RV park looked on. That gator eventually grabbed its inflatable prey and swam around a lake for three hours with it trapped between its teeth.

Brochures. Brochures from Florida Alligator Farms and Attractions. *Circa 1930s-1970s, $3-5.*

Florida Alligator Farms & Attractions

Florida has many roadside Alligator attractions. Some of these attractions simply have Alligators on display. In some of the larger attractions there are Alligators, Crocodiles, and other wild animals on display, as well as Alligator and wild animal shows, including Alligator wrestling. Some of the Alligator attractions are also Alligator farms where Alligators are raised for their hides and flesh. On some of these farms, thousands of Alligators are harvested each year.

Alligator farms and attractions are scattered throughout the state, most of which use some form of the word "Alligator" in their business names. Some of the farms and attractions (old and new) are:

Alligator Alley Wildlife Exhibits (Kissimmee), Alligator Farm (St. Andrews Bay), Alligator Joe's Farm (Palm Beach), Alligatorland Safari Zoo (Kissimmee), Big Bear Park (Largo), Casper's Ostrich & Alligator Farm (St. Augustine), Everglades Alligator Farm (Homestead), Everglades Gatorland (South Bay), Everglades Wonder Gardens (Bonita Springs), Florida Alligator Farm (Jacksonville), Florida Wild Animal & Reptile Ranch (St. Petersburg), Gatorama (Palmdale), Gator Jungle (Tampa), Gatorland (Orlando), Homosassa Springs (Homosassa), Jungle Adventures Nature Park & Zoo (Christmas), McKee Jungle Gardens (Vero Beach), Miracle Strip Jungle Land (Panama City), Musa Isle Seminole Indian Village (Miami), Native Village Wildlife Park (Hollywood), Okalee Indian Village (Hollywood), Ross Allen's Reptile Institute (Silver Springs), Sarasota Jungle Gardens, Sea Zoo (South Daytona), St. Augustine Alligator Farm, St. Petersburg Alligator Farm & Zoo, Tampa Alligator Farm (Sulphur Springs), Tropical Hobbyland Indian Village (Miami), Tropical Park (South Daytona), Weeki Wachee Springs (Weeki Wachee)

An Alligator Farm in Florida. Roadside Alligator farms and attractions are located throughout Florida. *Circa 1910, $3-5.*

St. Augustine Alligator Farm

In the early 1890s Everett C. Whitney developed a small curiosity and souvenir shop called the Burning Spring Museum on South Beach, which is now St. Augustine Beach. In 1893 Whitney, along with George Reddington and Felix Fire, opened the South Beach Alligator Farm next to the museum. Whitney ended his association with the South Beach Alligator Farm in 1903. Reddington was active for many years in his efforts to promote development of St. Augustine Beach. Although Reddington and Felix Fire were for some three decades equal partners in the operation of the Alligator Farm, Reddington was probably the more astute businessman of the two. The Farm was later renamed the St. Augustine Alligator Farm. Reddington became the sole owner in the early 1930s; however, Fire continued to work there until his retirement.

By 1910 the Alligator Farm had become an established Florida attraction. A 1916 St. Augustine guide publication said the attraction contained thousands of reptiles. During World War I thousands of soldiers were stationed near St. Augustine. When the war ended, many veterans decided to return to Florida, joining hundreds of thousands of other Americans in creating the Great Florida Land Boom of the 1920s. In 1937 Reddington sold the Farm to W. I. Drysdale and F. Charles Usina.

Hard working and aggressive businessmen, Drysdale and Usina promoted the facility locally and nationally, capitalizing on the public's fascination with Alligators. In 1937 they constructed a new "Mission Style" main building that contained offices, a gift shop, a taxidermy shop, and the entrance to the attraction. The Alligator Farm began to attract passengers from the Clyde Steamship Line in Jacksonville and soldiers from a nearby U.S. Army base in Starke. These visitors came from all parts of the nation and they consequently spread far and wide word about the museum with all the Alligators.

Drysdale and Usina began to improve the exhibits. An important addition to the reptile collection was purchased from Joseph Campbell of Jacksonville, reported to be Florida's first Alligator farmer. The Campbell acquisition gave them specimens from the three oldest Alligator attractions in Florida. In following years, they acquired collections from the Daytona Beach Alligator Farm, the Daytona Airport Zoo, and the North Miami Zoo. The attraction now not only contained Alligators, but also Crocodiles, ostriches, Galapagos turtles, monkeys, birds, and other Florida wildlife.

In the early 1970s David C. Drysdale, son of W. I. Drysdale, took over the operations and direction of the farm. In 1988 the St. Augustine Alligator Farm became one of a select list of zoological institutions throughout the United States. A year later the Alligator Farm purchased a large collection of reptiles, which included Gomek, a saltwater Crocodile that measured close to eighteen-feet in length and weighed over 1,700-pounds. Gomek, the largest known reptile on exhibit anywhere in the world, became the farm's star attraction until he died in 1997. A successor to Gomek was Maximo, a fifteen-foot, three-inch long, 1,250-pound Crocodile.

The St. Augustine Alligator Farm and Zoological Park has emerged in the twenty-first century as one of Florida's most popular attractions. However, the Park's central attraction is still the reptile that evolution has forgotten, the awesome Alligator.

Greetings from St. Augustine Alligator Farm. Handler Chris Lightburn wrestles an Alligator at the St. Augustine Alligator Farm. Lightburn was a skilled Alligator handler at the attraction for many years. *Circa 1960s, $2-4.*

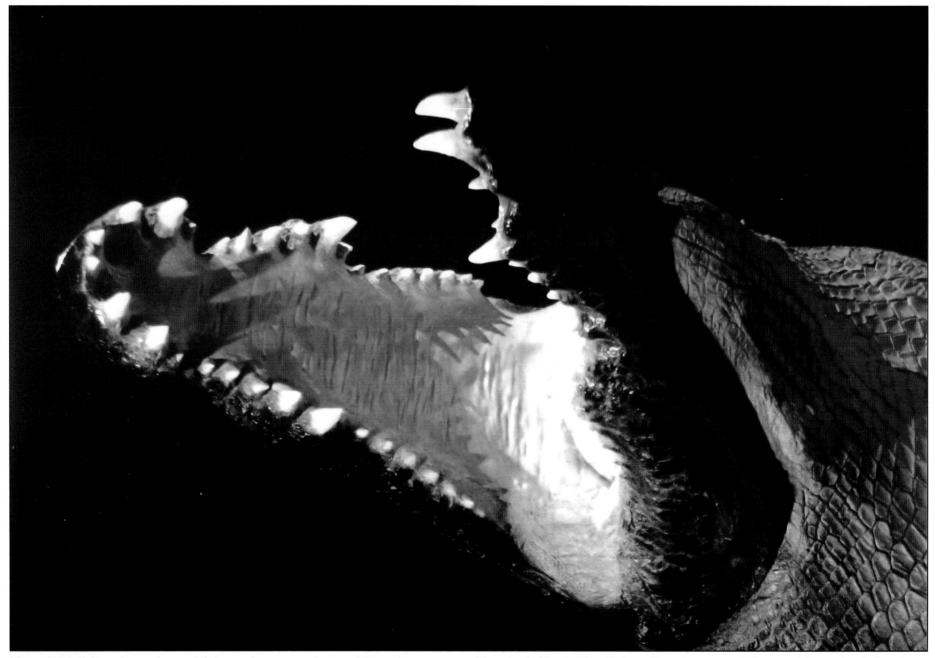

'Open Wide!' Gomek was the world's largest known reptile on exhibit and was housed in a special enclosure at the St. Augustine Alligator Farm designed to emulate his native habitat in New Guinea. Gomek measured close to eighteen feet in length and weighed over 1,700 pounds. *Circa 2000, $1-3.*

Gatorland

Long before the visionary eyes of Walt Disney turned Orlando into Mickey Mouse Land, Owen Godwin had a dream of his own. Gatorland, one of Florida's pioneer tourist attractions, is the fulfillment of that dream. Located between Orlando and Kissimmee, Gatorland has exhibited Alligators and other reptiles, birds, and animals for sixty years. As an operating Alligator farm, Gatorland sells the meat and hides of at least 1,000 Alligators a year. A portion of the money made from the sale of meat and leather products goes back into research on reptiles and to otherwise benefit the thousands of gators at Gatorland. The park, still owned by the Godwin family, has continued to grow through the years and is now a 770-plus-acre compound with thousands of reptile residents.

From a humble beginning with just a handful of Alligators and a few huts and pens made from cypress poles and thatched roofs, Godwin slowly built Gatorland (originally named "Snake Village and Alligator Farm") into a large Alligator attraction. Gatorland has entertained, educated, and amazed millions of visitors with animals from different parts of the world.

Casper is a thirteen-foot, five-inch-long, 997-pound Alligator at Gatorland. Casper joined the other reptiles at Gatorland in 2002, after he had obtained a long rap sheet of killing dogs in the Tampa Bay area.

Alligator Wrestling. You may picture Alligator wrestling as a bloodthirsty encounter—but it isn't. In most cases the Alligator simply wishes the handler would go away and let him sleep. Here, an animal trainer performs at Gatorland, an Alligator farm south of Orlando. *Circa 1990s, $1-3.*

Gatorama

Gatorama, located at 6180 Highway 27 in Palmdale, is one of Florida's first roadside Alligator attractions and reminds one of a tropical jungle. About 3,000 Alligators and 250 Crocodiles lurk about in this out-of-the-way property west of Lake Okeechobee. Giant oak and palm trees cover the fifteen-acre attraction. Monkeys, bobcats, raccoons, peacocks, ducks, and geese also call Gatorama home.

The star attraction at Gatorama is Goliath, a fourteen-foot, forty year old Crocodile. Goliath is the largest American Crocodile in the state. Other boarders at Gatorama are Salty, a fourteen-foot saltwater Crocodile; Rambo, a thirteen-foot Alligator; Mighty Mike, another thirteen-foot gator, and other Alligators and Crocodiles that have been there since Gatorama opened in 1957. Many of the Alligators and Crocodiles swim together in a lake.

The highlight of any Alligator roadside attraction is the feeding of the gators, and Gatorama is no exception. Chickens and pork ribs are fed to gators two times a day. The hungry mouths go through sixteen thousand pounds of meat a month. The owner of Gatorama, Allen Register, lost half a finger to one of his Crocodiles several years ago, when a hungry Croc took a bite as he was feeding her. Allen walks into a fenced-off gated platform and dangles huge slabs of ribs above the water. A Crocodile leaps half out of the

water to grab the meat. Visitors to Gatorama often capture this event with their cameras.

The Gatorama gift shop sells frozen gator meat in two-pound packages. What does it taste like: A *Miami Herald* story once described gator meat as "a cross between mahi-mahi and catfish with a sweet hint of clam." Patty, Allen's wife, has a favorite gator recipe—sautéed gator in garlic. One can also pick up recipes for honey-grilled gator ribs and Granny's Alligator chili at the gift shop.

In addition to being a tourist attraction, Gatorama is an operating Alligator farm and is the largest captive breeder in North America of the Acutus Crocodile.

Alligator Attraction. Gatorama, which opened in 1957, is located on U.S. Highway 27 in Palmdale, west of Lake Okeechobee and West Palm Beach. This roadside attraction has over 3,000 Alligators and Crocodiles. After watching the reptiles chow down, visitors can sample the Alligators themselves—the restaurant serves gator ribs and specialties made from Florida's other white meat. At Gatorama, a sign warns visitors: "No swimming or sunbathing. Violators may be eaten." *Circa 1960s, $4-6.*

Everglades Alligator Farm

Everglades Alligator Farm is a working Alligator farm at the edge of the Florida Everglades in Homestead (40351 S.W. 192 Avenue). The local Alligator population was in decline when the owners cleared seventy acres of land to create the farm. Over time, the farm was responsible for hatching and releasing up to one million Alligators and Crocodiles back into their natural habitats. The Everglades Farm offers educational wildlife shows and airboat tours in the Alligator- and snake-infested waters of the Everglades.

Jungle Adventures Nature Park & Zoo

The Jungle Adventures Nature Park & Zoo is located in Christmas, a small community on U.S. Highway 50 east of Orlando and west of Titusville. This Alligator farm has hundreds of Alligators, several Crocodiles, and other wild animals. A pontoon boat takes visitors on a jungle swamp lagoon past swimming gators, Alligators lying on the nearby shore, nesting birds, turtles, native Florida wildlife, an Indian village, and a replica of a sixteenth century Spanish Fort. The attraction also has a small restaurant and a gift shop. Visitors are able to get a close-up view of Goliath, a fifteen-foot long, 77-year old Alligator. Entrance to the Park is past Swampy, the largest concrete Alligator in Florida.

Alligator Farm Brochure. Brochure from the Everglades Alligator Farm in Homestead. *Circa 1990s, $1-3.*

'My What Big Teeth You Have!' Pictured is Swampy, the giant concrete Alligator entrance to Jungle Adventures Nature Park & Zoo in Christmas, a small community east of Orlando. *Circa 1990s, $1-3.*

36

Ross Allen's Reptile Institute

Ross Allen opened his Reptile Institute in 1940 in Central Florida at Silver Springs, near Ocala. This attraction housed one of the finest collections of Alligators, Crocodiles, snakes, and other wild animals in the country. One of the more colorful inhabitants was Old Cannibal. This twelve-foot long Alligator was captured by Allen near Webster after ranchers there said the large gator was killing their cattle. At the Institute Old Cannibal was put in a pen with thirteen smaller reptiles for company. One night he went on a rampage and killed the other Alligators. He was just plain mean. Old Cannibal was then kept in his own pen until he died in 1960.

Allen and his Alligators have appeared in over two dozen Grantland Rice Sportlight films, many news items, and a number of movies.

Hungry Gator. Left: "Old Cannibal," a one hundred-year-old, seven hundred-pound, twelve-foot long Alligator at the Reptile Institute at Silver Springs, was the meanest Alligator that Ross Allen had at his Institute. Old Cannibal killed thirteen smaller Alligators one night before being put in solitary confinement. *Circa 1940s, $1-3.*

Everglades Wonder Gardens

Everglades Wonder Gardens, located on the Tamiami Trail (U.S. Highway 41) in Bonita Springs, twenty-three miles south of Fort Myers, has been operated by Bill and Lester Piper since 1938. The Piper brothers had one of the biggest Alligators and Crocodile collections in Florida. They were especially proud of their Crocodile pool, which included thirty-two Crocodiles in one enclosure. "Dynamite," a fourteen-foot, three-inch long Crocodile, was the king of the pool.

In a separate pen was Big Joe, a twelve-foot long bad Crocodile that killed seven other Crocs over a period of a few months in 1949. The Alligator pool was full of large gators, scores of them ten to fourteen feet long and many of them caught by the Pipers themselves in the nearby Imperial River.

PART OF ONE OF THE ALLIGATOR POOLS

Alligator Pool. Shown is part of an Alligator pen at Everglades Wonder Gardens in Bonita Springs, north of Naples and twenty-three miles south of Fort Myers. *Circa 1930s, $2-4.*

Casper's Ostrich and Alligator Farm

Casper's Ostrich and Alligator Farm, located three miles north of St. Augustine on U.S. Highway 1, contained a large and interesting collection of ostriches, rare birds, Alligators, Crocodiles, and reptiles. Casper's opened as a roadside attraction in 1946. William Casper's Farm was always in the shadow of the established St. Augustine Alligator Farm on nearby Anastasia Island. Casper's never achieved the popularity of its neighbor despite being located on heavily traveled U.S. Highway 1. Casper's later changed its name to Casper's Alligator Jungle and in the 1970s simply to the Gatorland Alligator Farm.

Greetings from Casper's.
Postcard folder of Casper's Ostrich & Alligator Farm in St. Augustine. *Circa 1951, $3-5.*

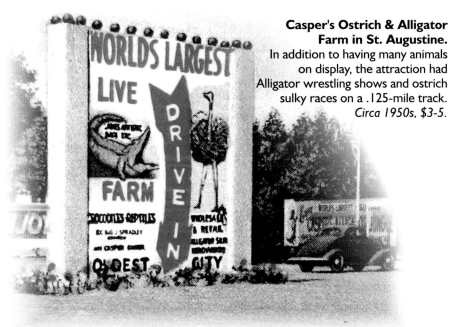

Casper's Ostrich & Alligator Farm in St. Augustine. In addition to having many animals on display, the attraction had Alligator wrestling shows and ostrich sulky races on a .125-mile track. *Circa 1950s, $3-5.*

Musa Isle Seminole Indian Village

The G. L. Stacey family established the Musa Isle Seminole Indian Village, located on the north fork of the Miami River, in 1922. Several Seminole Indian families lived at the village in palm-thatched "chickee" huts. The Seminole braves wrestled Alligators while the women sewed colorful shirts and skirts. In addition to about one hundred Alligators, the largest measured twelve-feet, the Village had eleven Crocodiles, the two largest being ten-feet long. The Alligator wrestling shows were favorite attractions for tourists visiting Miami.

Okalee Indian Village

The Okalee Indian Village, located twenty miles north of Miami on U.S. Highway 441 in Hollywood, was established in 1960. This fourteen-acre attraction had an arts and crafts center, a genuine Seminole village, and a deep-water Alligator wrestling pool. At this attraction a husky young Seminole plunged into a pool with a seven-foot Alligator, grappled with the reptile under water, hauled him to the surface, and piloted him ashore! Here the Indian wrestler climaxed the performance by wrestling his captive over on his back, whereupon the Alligator promptly passed out—a thing that never ceased to amaze visitors.

Florida Everglades

The Everglades, a shallow fifty-mile "river of grass," is a vast, complex water system that flows from Lake Okeechobee south more than one hundred miles to Florida Bay. Its 4.3 million acres contains a unique ecosystem of remarkable plants and animals found nowhere else on earth. Hundreds of Alligators can often be seen at Shark Valley in Everglades National Park. It is an excellent place to watch Alligator behavior. At Shark Valley, located on U.S. Highway 41 (Tamiami Trail) west of Miami, Park Rangers operate a fifteen-mile loop tram ride in the Everglades. The borrow pits at the observation tower are hangouts for Alligators, and the tower provides an opportunity to get more of a bird's-eye view – and a better understanding – of the Everglades landscape.

The Alligator has earned the title of "keeper of the Everglades." It cleans out the large holes dissolved in the Everglades' limestone bed and these functions as oasis in the dry winter season. Fish, turtles, snails, and other fresh water animals seek refuge in these life-rich solution holes, which become feeding grounds for Alligators, birds, and mammals until the rains return. Survivors, both predators and prey, then quit the holes to repopulate the Everglades.

M.136—Alligator Wrestling at Musa Isle Indian Village Miami, Florida

Musa Isle Indian Village, Miami, Florida. After visitors saw the thrilling and unusual exhibition of handling and wrestling Alligators, they would take a guided tour through the Musa Isle Indian Village. *Circa 1930s, $3-5.*

The landscape of the Everglades is as flat as a tabletop. Its highest point is only twenty-five feet above sea level. From Lake Okeechobee it tilts very slightly to the southwest, toward the Gulf of Mexico. The Everglades are based on lime rock that was once under the sea. The rock is filled with fossils of ancient sea creatures. In many parts of the Everglades, the rock is covered by peat, the remains of plants that partially decayed ages ago. The heart of the Everglades is a region of vast, flooded prairies, covered with tall sedge called saw grass, which grows often eleven feet or more.

Animal life in the Everglades is a mixture. More than two hundred species of fish have been found in the Everglades' waters. More than three hundred species of birds rest on tree limbs, paddle in the water, and fly overhead. More than forty species of mammals inhabit the great marsh. Among the rarest is the Florida panther. Other animals in the Everglades include deer, black bears, raccoons, rats, turtles, and snakes.

In the Everglades, however, the Alligator is king. Thousands of gators live in the saw grass prairies, sloughs, and culverts that pass under dirt roads in parts of the Everglades National Park.

Swimming Alligator. West along the Tamiami Trail (U.S. Highway 41) from Miami is found what Marjory Stoneman Douglas, Florida's most respected conservationist, describes as the great "river of grass"—the Everglades. This unusual subtropical ecosystem rally is a vast slow-moving shallow river that once covered the entire southern tip of Florida. Two million acres have been preserved for the pleasure of Alligators, birds, fish, and people who enjoy them. The Alligator has earned the title of "Keeper of the Everglades." The gator shown was photographed in the Shark Valley area of the Everglades. *Circa 2001, $1-3.*

Humorous Alligator Postcards

Alligators have often been the subjects of humorous Florida postcards. Confrontations with Alligators are a staple of Florida folklore, and the state itself was nicknamed the Alligator State.

A Fantasy Alligator Story

In the early nineteenth century someone in Eatonville, the home of writer Zora Neale Hurston and a neighboring community adjoining the northern boundary of Orlando, created a fantasy story. The story starts in Lake Belle, which is the home of Eatonville's most celebrated resident, the world's largest Alligator.

This legendary Alligator, it is said, is none other than a slave that escaped from a Georgia plantation and joined the Indians during the Seminole War. When the Indians retreated, he did not follow, but instead made 'big medicine' on the lakeshore, for he had been a celebrated conjuring man in Africa. He transformed himself into an Alligator, the god of his tribe, and slipped into the water. Now and then, people say, he resumes human form and roams the countryside about Eatonville. At such times all Alligators in the surrounding lakes bellow loudly all night long. 'The big one has gone back home,' whisper the villagers.

A Story of Alligators, Ducks, and Mosquitoes

Alligators like ducks. They find the spots in the marshes where the ducks huddle together at night and make a descent upon them. Frequently, while flocks of ducks are swimming in the deepest part of a river or lake, an Alligator will glide under the ducks and select those that suit him best. The ducks are drawn under the water so quietly that the flock is not alarmed for some time, and the Alligator manages to secure a square meal before he is suspected.

On summer nights the Alligator crawls to a chosen spot in the marshes. The air is filled with millions of mosquitoes. The reptile opens his enormous mouth and keeps his jaws apart until the inside of his mouth is black with the insects. Then he brings his jaws together with a snap, runs his tongue around the inside of his mouth, and swallows his winged visitors. He will keep this up until his appetite is satisfied.

From Bartram to Bond

In 1791 William Bartram wrote the following passage about Alligators in the St. Johns River:

IF NOTHING HAPPENS I'LL HAVE SOMETHING INTERESTING TO TELL YOU SOON

Comic Postcard. *Cancelled 1911, $3-5.*

"The Alligators were in such incredible numbers, and so close together from shore to shore, that it would have been easy to have walked across on their heads."

This vivid image so inspired a later screenwriter that it was actually attempted, without much success, using tethered reptiles in the James Bond film "Live and Let Die." The rented Alligators did not respond properly to this scene and the walk-on-Alligators' stuntman was injured. The botched scene made little impact in the completed movie.

Old Joe Murdered

Beloved Old Joe, famed Florida Alligator and long-time fixture of northwestern Florida's Wakulla Springs, never harmed man, woman, child, or dog. Roaming free in and around the picturesque springs for longer than anyone could remember, Old Joe was often sighted slumbering along the shoreline enjoying the crystal clear water and warm Florida sun.

Locals recall Old Joe being around long before the Wakulla Lodge was built in 1937. The eleven-foot, two-inch, 650-pound reptile was most active at night.

In August 1966, someone shot Old Joe. A $5,000 reward for information about Old Joe's assailant was never claimed.

I send you herewith the head of a Gator,
Watch for the mail—it will bring some more later.

Just Hanging Out.
Alligators were plentiful at the time Florida was discovered. With no enemies, other than Indians who killed some for food and hides, Alligators grew to enormous sizes, many reaching over nineteen feet in length. Today a thirteen-foot gator is considered a senior citizen. *Circa 1990s, $1-3.*

A HUNGRY ALLIGATOR IN FLORIDA   FF 90

A Hungry Gator in Florida. The Alligator, like all creatures of nature, has his place in our ecological system. During times of drought their wallowed out "gator-holes" are a source of water for other wildlife. The Alligator helps to control the population of other animals including fish and snakes. Gator holes are an important part of a swamp. Mud and plants pushed aside by the Alligator become rich soil where new, healthy plants grow. During a drought, or dry period, a gator hole still holds water. It's home to both the Alligator and its young. Fish, birds, and other animals live in and near the gator hole, too. They may stay until the rain returns. But sometimes, the guests become dinner! *Circa 1930s, $1-3.*

A Native of Florida

A Native of Florida. Alligators make a contribution to their habitats that benefit others. They feed and excrete in the water, which may help to recycle nutrients for plants on which fish feed. They open up trails and help to keep waterways open through marshlands. They deepen waterholes during droughts and provide a habitat for other animals. *Cancelled 1909, $4-6.*

Florida Pets, Alligators taking a Sun Bath.

Florida Pets.

The Alligator is probably the most picturesque and popular feature of the Florida peninsula. Alligators are truly wild and dangerous animals that deserve the respect of humans. They have big teeth and their jaw muscles are so powerful that the strongest person on earth cannot pull them apart. Their jaws can slam shut with as much pressure as 2,000 pounds per square inch. *Circa 1914, $1-3.*

873 ONE OF THE EARLY FLORIDA NATIVES AT HOME IN THE EVERGLADES

One of the early Florida Natives.

American Alligator populations declined sharply in the early 1960s after decades of intense hunting. The Alligator populations rebounded so well in the 1980s that Alligator meat started being sold. Here, an Alligator basks in the sun in the Florida Everglades. *Circa 1930s, $3-5.*

"LONGING" FOR YOU IN FLORIDA—F176

"Longing" for you in Florida—F176.

The large, pink, fleshy fold at the back of the Alligator's mouth stops water entering the breathing passages when it's underwater. By opening its mouth above the water the Alligator allows water to evaporate into the air and cools itself down. The upper jaw of Alligators is almost solid bone and has little flexibility. However, between the toothsome rims of the lower jaw the skin is loose and elastic. *Circa 1930s, $3-5.*

"Look Pleasant." The Alligator has been called the most valuable wild animal in Florida. About 50,000 German tourists came to Florida in 1989 to enjoy the weather and see two things: the space vehicles at Cape Canaveral and the Alligators. Here, a tourist takes a photograph of several Alligators. *Circa 1908, $5-7.*

Who Said Dinner? The Florida Alligator is found throughout the state, being most numerous in the Florida Everglades. They inhabit the swamp recesses usually near streams, rivers, or lakes. However, they have been found in built-up urban areas such as Miami, Fort Lauderdale, Orlando, and Tampa. *Cancelled 1908, $5-7.*

A Ravenous Pair.

Florida Alligators

Florida Alligators. Alligators sunning themselves on a sandbar in a Florida river. The Alligator's body is suited for life on land and in water. The Alligator uses its short, stocky legs for walking. In the water it swims by sweeping its tail from side to side. *Cancelled 1909, $3-5.*

A Ravenous Pair. Humans and Alligators differ considerably about "killing." Humans kill for sport (presumably to confirm their dominion over other creatures) or simply for trinkets and souvenirs (the tangible evidence of domination). Alligators qualify as a target for these purposes. But Alligators kill nothing for sport and do not normally attack humans for food or for any other reason without provocation. Humans destroy more Alligators than any other predator does. Nesting females are often killed and their nests destroyed by hunters. Many Alligators are shot because they are thought to be dangerous. *Circa 1908, $5-7.*

Alligator at Home, Florida.

r one of these. ge
three ful lon
oun here.

Sunbathing.

Many Alligators are found with empty stomachs. Scientists believe that hatchlings can survive up to four months without eating and adults may last a year between meals. They also eat very little during the winter when they are sluggish and inactive. This Gator sunning near a pond bank is nine feet long. Imagine one fourteen feet in length. *Cancelled 1905, $3-5.*

G 15548 A reputable citizen of Florida.

We have one of these gentlemen alive, he is about three ful long. We like it very much down here. Your friend, Dr. Banker.

A Reputable Citizen of Florida.

Alligators will not eat when temperatures drop below about sixty degrees Fahrenheit because there is not enough heat to activate their digestive enzymes. Cold weather can kill an Alligator with a full stomach, for the food will rot instead of digest. *Cancelled 1907, $4-6.*

Waiting for the Kill. Alligators are opportunists. They usually don't go hunting for their food—they wait for it to come to them. They have nothing but time. They're on permanent stakeout. Most of the time Alligators are in no hurry to do anything. *Circa 1908, $3-5.*

NO. 265

A NATIVE FLORIDIAN.

E. C. KROPP- PUBL- MILWAUKEE, NO. *1755*

A Native Floridian. Alligators appear slow and docile, but they can be fast and aggressive, especially when hungry. It is said that an Alligator can outrun a horse for a distance of thirty feet. A large Alligator can grab a one hundred-pound hog and crush its head like a potato chip, spraying its brains twenty-five feet. The jaws of an Alligator are a crushing machine ideal for crushing turtle and crab shells. *Circa 1904, $3-5.*

Smile for the Camera! An Alligator has around eighty very sharp teeth and a tail that is also very dangerous. His method of attack is to knock his victim down with a swat of the tail while almost simultaneously grabbing with his vice-like jaws. If possible, he will knock the victim into the water where the reptile is more at home. This Alligator's dental display gives some appreciation of the power of its bite. This Alligator was photographed on the Silver River in central Florida. *Circa 1940s, $3-5.*

An Alligator in Everglades National Park. This park is a mysterious wilderness of mangrove swamps, cypress trees, and sawgrass. It is one of the Alligator's strongholds where he lives in sawgrass so sharp that old-time trappers and hunters often used copper wire laces in their boots to offset its razor-like edges. *Cancelled 1921, $3-5.*

On the Prowl. Food for an Alligator can be anything that it can out-swim, ambush, or overpower. One zoologist cut open a dead Alligator's stomach and found several pieces of wood, a fishing sinker, and a crumpled can. The Alligator had swallowed these things to help grind the coarse food it could not chew. Most of the time an Alligator will eat his food in the water. *Circa 1940s, $3-5.*

S-80 A NATIVE OF ST. PETERSBURG, FLORIDA, THE SUNSHINE CITY.

A Native of St. Petersburg, Florida. The Sunshine City. When an Alligator is on land, it usually moves very slowly, but it can also run very fast if he is after something. The Alligator's legs are extremely short in comparison with its body, but they can lift its body clear of the ground. This view shows the "crooked, toothy smile" of the Alligator. *Cancelled 1950, $2-4.*

A Bevy of Gators. Young Alligators frequently gather together for mutual protection. When the Alligator hatches from the egg, it is only six to seven inches long, but will grow one foot a year for the next four to five years. After this its growth will be much slower, until it reaches a length of about thirteen feet. The Alligator will eat almost anything, including fish, turtles, snakes, and eggs. The large ones can go for a year without food or water, but usually eat once a week and can eat up to fifty pounds of food at one time. It takes a few days for them to digest their food. *Circa 1930s, $3-5.*

Alligators Enjoying the Florida Sunshine. Alligators are adapted primarily to aquatic habitats of Florida. They roam from one area to another during courtship or when the areas they inhabit become overcrowded by humans or other dominant Alligators. At breeding time, March and April, an Alligator will travel more than one hundred miles looking for a mate. The eggs are laid during the last week of May or June. *Circa 1920s, $3-5.*

291 ALLIGATORS ENJOYING THE FLORIDA SUNSHINE

50

ALBINO ALLIGATOR. VERY RARE.

A Rare One! Little gators are so cute! This is an albino Alligator. There are also Alligators that are white, however they are not albino. They are what are known as leucistic animals. This means they lack pigment in the skin like albino, but have color in the eyes. An albino's eyes are pink, showing the tiny blood vessels below the surface, but the leucistic Alligator has blue eyes. *Circa 1940s, $3-5.*

Leucistic Alligator. This Alligator, with its brilliant white skin and smoky blue eyes, is a leucistic Alligator. Leucism differs from albinism in that pigment is lacking in the skin, but not in the eyes. Albinos, on the other hand, have no pigment in the eyes, resulting in a pink color (the tiny blood vessels below the surface show through). This view shows a white Alligator at Silver Springs. *Circa 1980s, $1-3.*

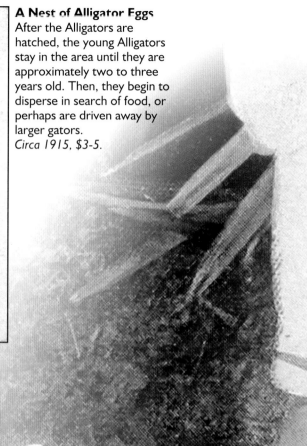

A Nest of Alligator Eggs

After the Alligators are hatched, the young Alligators stay in the area until they are approximately two to three years old. Then, they begin to disperse in search of food, or perhaps are driven away by larger gators. *Circa 1915, $3-5.*

A NEST OF ALLIGATOR EGGS, FLORIDA.

Alligator Egg Hatching in Florida 246

Alligator Egg Hatching in Florida. Reared in artificial surroundings, the growth rate of young Alligators is invariably better than that of wild stock. Ultimately, males will continue to grow at a faster rate than females and will be correspondingly larger. Young Alligators, as shown in this view, are relatively colorful compared to adults, usually having a number of yellow stripes on their bodies that fade after a time. When grown, the Alligator is dull gray and dark olive in color. *Circa 1930s, $2-4.*

Alligator Eggs Hatching, St. Petersburg, Fla.

Alligator Eggs Hatching, St. Petersburg, Florida. Alligator farms capitalize on the reproductive capacity of the female Alligator. In the wild, if forty-five eggs are laid, the majority of hatchlings die at an early stage. But in a controlled environment, a very high percentage of the youngsters can be reared satisfactorily and, ultimately, its meat and hides can be sold. *Circa 1912, $3-5.*

Alligators Hatching from the Eggs. As young Alligators get ready to hatch, they will begin to make high-pitched, grunting sounds. The female Alligator responds to these calls by using her mouth and forefeet to remove the nesting material covering the young, thus liberating the six- to nine-inch hatchlings from the nest. The first two years are the most critical in the life of a gator. Eighty percent or more may fall victim to wading birds, otters, snakes, raccoons, skunks, bobcats, bears, large fish, and even larger Alligators. Once an Alligator exceeds four feet, it is relatively safe from predators (other than humans), but still may be vulnerable to cannibalism. *Cancelled 1925, $2-4.*

A Youngling. Young Alligators eat insects, crayfish, snails, tadpoles, water bugs, spiders, frogs, and small fish. At a length of about six feet, they begin to feed predominantly on turtles, fish, snakes, water birds, and small mammals. Larger Alligators occasionally take deer, hogs, and domestic calves. Like their parents, young Alligators are cold-blooded and regulate their body temperature through a variety of behaviors. Here, a brightly colored Alligator basks in the sun. Basking is an important part of the Alligator's lifestyle, enabling it to raise its body temperature under the sun's rays when the water is relatively cool. *Circa 1940s, $1-3.*

Alligators on the Banks of a Florida Swamp.
Just a few years ago, illegal hunting and encroaching civilization had all but destroyed the Alligator population in the South. They were added to the endangered species list in the United States. Now Alligators have made a comeback. Conservationists intent on preserving this legendary reptile helped the Alligator get back on its feet. Once again Florida swamps, marshes, and rivers are teeming with Alligators.
Circa 1910, $1-3.

ALLIGATOR ON THE BANKS OF A FLORIDA SWAMP

Going for a Swim?
In addition to audible signals—growls, grunts, bellows, jaw clamps, roars, and head slaps—Alligators also communicate by generating sub audible vibrations (sounds below the hearing level of humans).
Circa 1990s, $2-4.

Gator's Ashore! An Alligator does not have a brain, but rather a cerebral cortex or brain stem. They are instilled with a predator intelligence that has enabled them to outlive dinosaurs. They are smart and highly adaptive to changing environments. This view also shows that they have enormous mouths. On hot days Alligators laze around with their mouths open wide; they are letting moisture evaporate to help them cool down. An Alligator can lie in the sun with its mouth open for hours. *Circa 1940s, $2-4.*

Beautiful Florida.
Alligator in Native Wilds.

A Gator Lying on a Log. Alligators seek suitable habitats where they can feed, bask in the sun, perform courtship dances, nest, mate, and watch over their young. They are an enduring participant of the Florida landscape, though they cannot live on dry land. *Circa 1940s, $1-3.*

The Rapids on Miami River. Alligators are fearless hunters. They will go after just about anything that comes near the water. And they are so strong that most animals are helpless against them. As soon as an Alligator manages to grab hold of its prey with its muscular jaws and pull it underwater, the animal is probably doomed. This Alligator is at the headwaters of the Miami River. *Cancelled 1906, $4-6.*

The Rapids on Miami River, Fla.

Hide and Seek.
Alligators often remain largely hidden, resembling, for example, logs in the water. They can move very close to the shore, seizing prey as it comes to drink. *Circa 2002, $1-3.*

A Mature Gator. Size rather than age is significant in determining sexual maturity in Alligators. These reptiles grow at different rates through their range, and those found in cooler northern areas grow more slowly and mature later than their southern counterparts. *Circa 1990s, $1-3.*

The Reptilian Cyrano de Bergerac? Not many people think of either the Alligator or Crocodile as a handsome reptile—unless they compare it with a gavial! The gavial, with its broom handle-like nose, is the oddest looking of all the crocodilians. Except for catching fish, the gavial tends to be quite shy. Several Florida Alligator farms and attractions have gavials on display. *Circa 1990s, $1-3.*

Guarding its Territory. Alligators are often territorial, particularly during the mating season. If another animal enters an Alligator's territorial domain, the resident sends a very unambiguous signal, a threat that 'I'm getting ready to attack.' Threat is a much more economical way of defending a territory than actual fighting because it requires less effort and poses no risk to the defender. *Circa 1940s, $1-3.*

A Submerged Gator. The Alligator can float submerged, with only its eyes and back showing. Its valves keep water out of its ears and nose. Without making any commotion, it can sneak up on its prey. They like to eat dogs, cats, and raccoons—almost all small animals. There have been many instances of owners walking their small dogs by the side of a lake and having the pet pulled in by an Alligator. *Circa 1960s, $3-5.*

A Florida Crocodile.

Alligator look-alike, the Crocodile. What is the difference between an Alligator and a Crocodile? The most striking difference is the shape of the head. The Alligator has a broad, rounded snout, while the Crocodile snout is narrower and more pointed. Adult Alligators are gray-black, while the Crocodile is yellowish-gray in color. The Crocodile has olive eyes while the Alligator's eyes are charcoal. Naturalist Dr. William Hornaday discovered the Crocodile in Florida in 1875 near Biscayne Bay in Miami. As living relics of prehistory, Crocodiles arouse fear and fascination. *Circa 1910s, $3-5.*

The Crocodile. A small population of American Crocodiles live in the southern part of Florida, being found mainly in the Florida Keys and the Everglades. *Circa 1920s, $1-3.*

Miss Alli-Gator, Florida.

Lurking in the Tall Grass.
Even though the Alligator is well equipped for both surface and underwater travel, his favorite method of locomotion is to scull his way through the water, rhythmically wagging his tail from side to side while holding his short legs close to his body. He uses these same hand-like webbed paws to paddle about and balance himself when floating in water for long periods of time.
Circa 1910, $5-7.

Chapter Two: **Alligator Hunting**

I promised some more—here is the next part,
Save this as well and await the third Card.

Shooting the Alligators. In the 1800s many visitors to Florida would amuse themselves by shooting Alligators from the deck of a Steamboat. Even John J. Audubon, an early nineteenth century naturalist, found Alligator hunting to be suitable entertainment for visitors. The wood engraving shown, titled, "Shooting Alligators from a Steamboat on the Ocklawaha River," was published in a *Scribner's Monthly* magazine. *Circa 1874, $5-7.*

Alligator Hunting. Regional guidebooks pointed out the best spots to find Alligators. One 1885 guidebook stated, "There are still enough to furnish the sportsman with plenty of good game. You will have no difficulty in finding as many Alligators as you want." *Circa 1885, $5-7.*

Hunters Seek their Prey. In summer, when water levels were high in the Everglades and swamps, the hunters took Alligators by the tens of thousands; between 1880 and 1894 they killed at least 2.5 million of the big reptiles. Hundreds of thousands more were lost when nests were raided to satisfy national demand for baby Alligators. This view illustrates the return from a successful Alligator hunt. *Circa 1908, $12-14.*

AN ALLIGATOR HUNTER, FLORIDA

An Alligator Hunter. Alligator hunting was a lucrative pursuit for some Florida pioneers. Alligator steaks were considered a delicacy and their skins were in great demand by leather goods manufacturers in the north. The Alligator has been used to produce every kind of tourist item imaginable. They have been stuffed and skinned, their hides turned into handbags, fashionable shoes and belts, their claws as purses, their teeth as jewelry, and their eggs as curios. *Cancelled 1933, $5-7.*

62

A New Family Pet? A 1908 Alligator hunt resulted in Bird Latham, manager of the St. Petersburg Electric Light and Power Company (he's holding the rope around the gator's snout), and associates bringing home this captured reptile. *Cancelled 1916, $8-10.*

A Prize Catch. An Alligator hunter poses with the kill from a hunt on Lake Panasoffkee. On this hunt thirty Alligators were taken, ranging in size from twelve inches to twelve feet in length. *Circa 1920, $5-7.*

Bringing Gator Home. Alligators have been hunted for meat and skins since humans first set foot in Florida. Alligator skins were sold in the Miami area for $7 each as early as 1800. There is little doubt Alligators were overexploited largely because of the demand for Alligator leather. *Circa 1920s, $10-12.*

9227. "ALLIGATOR JOE," AND HIS PETS, PALM BEACH, FLA.   COPYRIGHT, 1904, BY DETROIT PHOTOGRAPHIC CO.

Playing with his Pets. "Alligator Joe" works with Alligators at his Palm Beach Alligator Farm. This farm was one of Palm Beach's first tourist attractions. "Alligator Joe" Frazier was a man with an eye for women as well as for gators. Local legend has it that he had nine wives. Circus acts were also performed at this Alligator Farm. Seminole Indians wrestled Alligators and Crocodiles and sometimes Joe would shoot a gator to the delight of the tourists. *Copyright 1904, $8-10.*

Landing an Alligator on Dock, Florida.

Posing With a Captured Alligator. *Circa 1910, $6-8.*

Florida Alligator Hunter

Florida Alligator Hunter. Capturing a wild Alligator weighing a half-ton was no job for amateurs. There are many different ways to catch Alligators. Lassoing with a lariat is one way. Snag hooks, harpoons, and bait hooks suspended over water are other methods. *Cancelled 1913, $8-10.*

8228 "ALLIGATOR JOE'S" BUNGALOW IN THE JUNGLE, FLA.   COPYRIGHT, 1904, BY DETROIT PHOTOGRAPHIC CO.

Alligator Joe's Bungalow in the Jungle. It was reported that Alligator Joe, for a fee, would take a party of tourists into the Everglades for a day, guaranteeing that he would find an Alligator for them to shoot. It was rumored that an accomplice was always sent ahead to free the Alligator at the proper moment, after the hunters had been paddled by a devious course to the selected spot. Here is Alligator Joe's hunting bungalow in the Florida jungle. *Copyright 1904, $3-5.*

Crocodile caught by Alligator Joe, Florida.

Crocodile Caught. Here is "Alligator Joe" Frazier—after capturing a Crocodile to add to his Alligator Farm collection. *Circa 1900s, $8-10.*

White Tiger with his Alligators.
This postcard, part of the Florida
Artistic Series, was published by M.
mark in Jacksonville. White Tiger is
a Seminole Indian Alligator wrestler.
The card was printed in Germany.
Circa 1905, $8-10.

A Captured Alligator. This was a common sight until the 1960s. In 1961, the
Florida Game and Fresh Water Fish Commission stopped the hunting season for the
giant reptile and provided full protection for it. Despite the complete protection
of Alligators under this law, extensive Alligator poaching continued until 1970. At
that time, an amendment to the federal Lacey Act made the interstate shipment
of illegally taken Alligators a federal violation. This act, combined with the reduced
demand for Alligator skins resulting from a decline in many traditional retail markets,
virtually eliminated poaching. The Alligator is still protected in Florida, but is no longer
endangered. The state now has annual licensed Alligator hunts. *Cancelled 1915, $5-7.*

Luring the Gator. Deep in the Florida Everglades, Seminole Indians capture a live,
fighting Alligator using tricks handed down from generation to generation. The Indians
used to trade Alligator hides for grits and bacon. *Circa 1960s, $1-3.*

"Waiting for a Gator,"
Florida.

"Waiting for a Gator." This gun-packing lady is looking for an Alligator to shoot. *Circa 1910, $3-5.*

Gator Shooting, Upper St. Johns River. An 1890s Alligator hunt on the Upper St. Johns River. A photo reproduction postcard. *Circa 1980s, $1-3.*

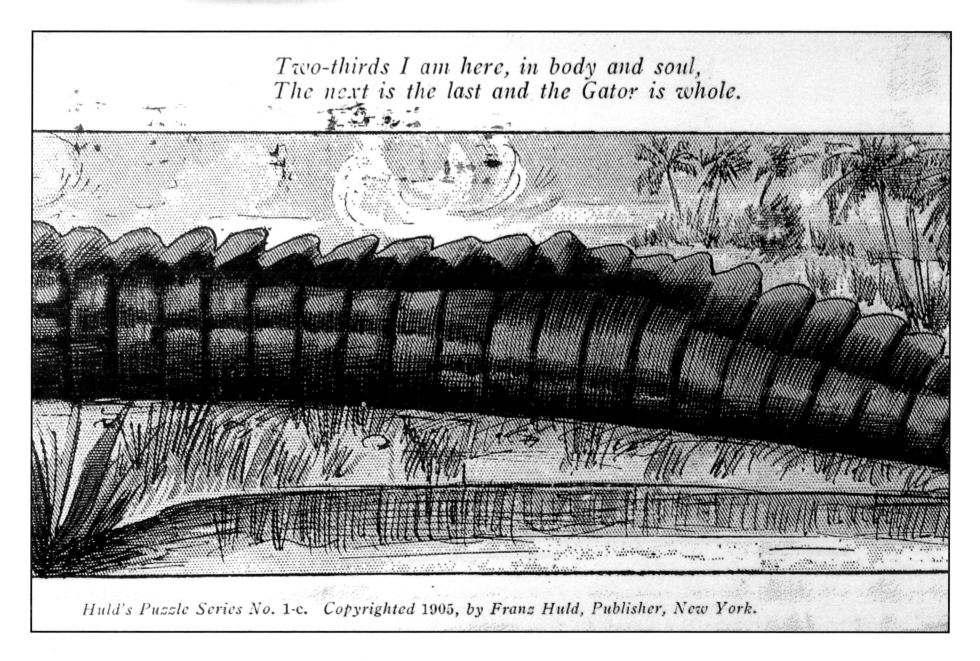

Two-thirds I am here, in body and soul,
The next is the last and the Gator is whole.

Huld's Puzzle Series No. 1-c. Copyrighted 1905, by Franz Huld, Publisher, New York.

Her Pets. Feeding time is always frantic at an Alligator Farm. The gators anxiously await their next meal. This view shows a lady feeding "her pets" at an Alligator farm in Jacksonville. These Alligators don't want to fight anyone or anything—all they want to do is eat, eat, eat! *Circa 1911, $4-6.*

Feeding Time at the Alligator Farm. Feeding time at this Alligator Farm was one of the more interesting sights. Alligators are cold-blooded, flesh-eating reptiles that are fed many pounds of fish each week. Large Alligators can swallow their food whole. On Alligator farms, the main goal is to raise the animals as quickly as possible. Alligators being raised for harvest are fed a special formula each day. One such formula is a mixture of red meat, chicken liver, and vitamins. Feeding time is happy time for always-hungry gators. *Circa 1912, $4-6.*

A LIVELY BUNCH OF ALLIGATORS, FLORIDA.

A Lively Bunch! In the late nineteenth century a new form of reptilian tourist attraction was born—the Alligator Farm. Alligator farms were soon providing the scientific community with easily obtained specimens, and amazing travelers with masses of caged 'gators.' *Circa 1910s, $3-5.*

70

BASKING IN THE SUNSHINE. These are some of the Breeding Stock, 25 to 100 years old. These are the Alligators that lay from 40 to 60 eggs each, from which thousands of Baby Alligators are hatched yearly. THE FLORIDA ALLIGATOR FARM, Jacksonville, Florida. The Largest Alligator Farm in the World.

Basking in the Sun. In the early 1900s, the Florida Alligator Farm in Jacksonville was one of the largest gator farms in the world. *Circa 1910, $3-5.*

Alligator Farm, South Jacksonville. Alligators generally become aroused only in the presence of food or physical threat and otherwise prefer to laze in the water or lie about near it, like these residents of the Florida Alligator Farm in South Jacksonville. They are quite social as they take their daily sun. *Cancelled 1923, $3-5.*

Gators Bask in the Sun. Alligators basking in the sun at the Florida Alligator Farm in Jacksonville. Largely nocturnal, gators do most of their moving around at night. *Cancelled 1916, $3-5.*

BASKING IN THE SUN AT THE ALLIGATOR FARM, JACKSONVILLE, FLA.

Pablo Queen. This view shows Pablo Queen, a 784-pound gator at the Florida Alligator Farm, located on the south bank of St. Johns River. *Circa 1912, $3-5.*

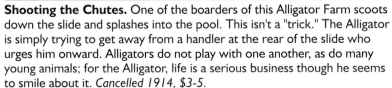

Shooting the Chutes. One of the boarders of this Alligator Farm scoots down the slide and splashes into the pool. This isn't a "trick." The Alligator is simply trying to get away from a handler at the rear of the slide who urges him onward. Alligators do not play with one another, as do many young animals; for the Alligator, life is a serious business though he seems to smile about it. *Cancelled 1914, $3-5.*

"Big Joe" Alligator, Jacksonville, Florida. *Circa 1908, $3-5.*

Alligator Farm, Florida.

Mr. and Mrs. "Alligator Joe" (CAMPBELL) Jacksonville, Fla.

Mr. & Mrs. "Alligator Joe." Mr. and Mrs. Joseph Campbell, owners of the Florida Alligator Farm in Jacksonville, were better known as Mr. and Mrs. "Alligator Joe." In 1891 Alligator Joe Campbell opened the Florida Alligator Farm on what is now the site of Prudential Insurance Co.'s modern skyscraper office building in South Jacksonville. *Circa 1910s, $8-10.*

Alligator Farm, Florida. This view illustrates Palm Beach's "Alligator Joe" sucking Alligator eggs for breakfast. Alligator eggs are bright white, oval, and about three inches long. Wouldn't it be comical to see how Alligator Joe would fit into today's Palm Beach elite society? *Cancelled 1911, $6-8.*

"Alligator Joe" Frazier's Farm in Palm Beach. This undivided-back Raphael Tuck & Sons postcard was printed in Holland. *Circa 1904, $5-7.*

A Florida Alligator Farm.

"A Florida Alligator Farm"

A Florida Alligator Farm. Shown is "Alligator Joe" Frazier's Alligator Farm in Palm Beach. The Everglades Club was built on this site in 1920. The club, designed by Addison Mizner and built by Paris Singer, began in 1918 as a hospital for convalescing World War I veterans. The war ended before the hospital could be completed. Singer suggested that Mizner redesign it as a club. Over the years the Everglades Club had undergone considerable changes. *Cancelled 1908, $4-6.*

SA-6—One of the Breeding Pens at Casper's Alligator Jungle, St. Augustine, Fla.

Gatorland. Casper's opened as a roadside attraction in the mid-1940s. This U.S. Highway 1 Alligator attraction later became the Gatorland Alligator Farm, which operated until 1982. *Circa 1970s, $1-3.*

A Breeding Pen. Alligators start breeding usually from the age of eight to thirteen years. These valued specimens are only a few of the many at Casper's Ostrich & Alligator Farm in St. Augustine. When hungry, these reptiles can be very active and hostile. Otherwise, except during the breeding season, they are about as lazy as a sloth. Casper's later changed its name to Casper's Alligator Jungle and in the 1970s simply to the Gatorland Alligator Farm. *Circa 1940s, $2-4.*

SA-7—"Old Columbus" at Casper's Alligator Jungle, St. Augustine, Fla.

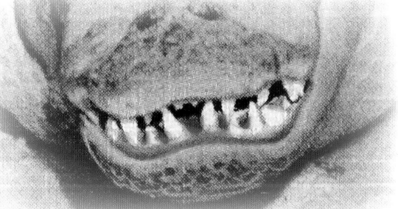

"Old Columbus." Look out! Here comes "Old Columbus," a large Alligator at Casper's Ostrich & Alligator Farm in St. Augustine. This was a very popular tourist attraction in the 1950s. As shown, several of the Alligator's teeth become quite large with age. Very old Alligators however lose most of their teeth. An Alligator's teeth are not made for chewing, but for catching and holding their prey. *Cancelled 1952, $4-6.*

Whitney's Ponce de Leon Spring, St. Augustine.
In the 1890s a museum of marine curiosities was located on Anastasia Island in St. Augustine. Part of this museum was Everett C. Whitney's "Burning Spring." Whitney's attraction was simply an artesian well pouring forth highly sulfuric water. Mixed with gasoline and ignited, the stream issued a blue flame, a phenomenon that seemed unexplainable to the visitors who observed it. The burning spring remained a fixture at the attraction for years. In 1893 George Reddington, Felix Fire, and Whitney opened the South Beach Alligator Farm next to the museum. This farm later became the St. Augustine Alligator Farm. *Circa early 1900s, $18-20.*

Greetings from St. Augustine Alligator Farm. The St. Augustine Alligator Farm is listed on the National Register of Historic Places. It has the world's largest collection of Alligators and Crocodiles. At this attraction on Anastasia Island, two miles south of the Bridge of Lions, visitors can explore the habitat of Alligators, Crocodiles, giant tortoises, birds, and snakes. The farm, established in 1893, has always been one of Florida's favorite attractions. The "Mission" style main building of the St. Augustine Alligator Farm, shown here, has been a landmark along U.S. Highway A1A for more than seventy years. It was built in 1937. *Circa 1945, $1-3.*

St. Augustine Alligator Farm. For over a century, visitors to the St. Augustine Alligator Farm have thrilled to the sight of its ferocious looking Alligators. They generally become aroused only in the presence of food or physical threat and otherwise prefer to laze in the water or lay about near it. *Circa 1950s, $2-4.*

76

Reddington's "Gator" Farm, Florida.
The South Beach Alligator Farm in St. Augustine Beach contained four times as many large live Alligators as any other collection in the world and had them ranging in size from the newly-hatched to Old Ponce, the largest and probably the oldest Alligator in captivity. This was also the home of Old Jack, often called the meanest Alligator on earth. This farm later became the St. Augustine Alligator Farm. *Circa 1911, $3-5.*

Sunbathing. The owners of the St. Augustine Alligator Farm, W. I. Drysdale and Charlie Usina, arranged weekend tours of the Alligator Farm for troops stationed at a nearby military camp. On weekends during the World War II years, the attraction was invariably packed with military visitors. They came from all parts of the nation and they consequently spread far and wide word about the museum with all the Alligators. This view shows the main breeding pool. *Circa 1930s, $1-3.*

Performing for the Crowd. Curator Greg Lepera feeding Gomek. Feeding time came twice a week. From a safe vantage point on a walkway above the water, the keeper held out the carcasses of skinned nutria, a South American rodent that resembles a muskrat. Gomek came straight up out of the water to grab the food, opening his huge jaws like the hood of a car, gulping great chunks of the meat whole. He could eat one hundred pounds of meat at a single feeding. *Circa 1991, $1-3.*

Roseate Spoonbills. Alligators are not the only reason people visit the St. Augustine Alligator Farm. Birds are an important part of this landmark attraction. The farm's two-acre real-Florida swamp habitat is the breeding ground for several water birds to nest and raise their young every spring. The wild bird rookery is in full breeding plumage from mid-March to July. Herons, egrets, ibis, roseate spoonbills, and wood storks find comfort in building their nests in the trees, with Alligators, below, provide protection from natural predators such as opossums, snakes, and raccoons. Shown is a roseate spoonbill nest. *Circa 1940s, $1-3.*

Brochures. Brochures from the St. Augustine Alligator Farm. *Circa 1930s-1990s, $3-5.*

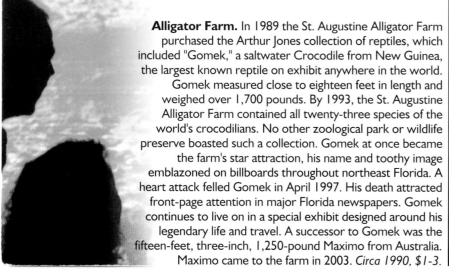

Alligator Farm. In 1989 the St. Augustine Alligator Farm purchased the Arthur Jones collection of reptiles, which included "Gomek," a saltwater Crocodile from New Guinea, the largest known reptile on exhibit anywhere in the world. Gomek measured close to eighteen feet in length and weighed over 1,700 pounds. By 1993, the St. Augustine Alligator Farm contained all twenty-three species of the world's crocodilians. No other zoological park or wildlife preserve boasted such a collection. Gomek at once became the farm's star attraction, his name and toothy image emblazoned on billboards throughout northeast Florida. A heart attack felled Gomek in April 1997. His death attracted front-page attention in major Florida newspapers. Gomek continues to live on in a special exhibit designed around his legendary life and travel. A successor to Gomek was the fifteen-feet, three-inch, 1,250-pound Maximo from Australia. Maximo came to the farm in 2003. *Circa 1990, $1-3.*

Brochures from Gatorland. *Circa 1940s-1990s, $3-5.*

A Tropical Paradise? The sub-tropical setting and climate at Gatorland is ideal for raising Alligators. Breeding pens, baby Alligator nurseries, and rearing ponds are located throughout the seventy-acre park. Bridges and walkways are designed to permit visitors an opportunity to observe and study the fascinating life of the Alligator. In many areas the visitor can actually feed the Alligators and Crocodiles. The Alligators shown here are on an island at Gatorland. *Cancelled d1964. $2-4.*

Open Wide! Founded in 1948, Owen Godwin's Gatorland between Orlando and Kissimmee began with a handful of Alligators and a few huts and pens made from cypress poles and thatched roots. Today, the Alligator Farm, which was originally named "Snake Village and Alligator Farm," displays thousands of Alligators. The signature icon of Gatorland: the gaping jaws of a huge concrete and steel Alligator head entranceway, was designed and built in 1962 by Frank Godwin, Owen's son. This one-of-a-kind entrance, known the world over, has welcomed millions of visitors. Postcard photo by Clinton H. Ruth. *Circa 1960s, $3-5.*

A Gator Adventure.
Jungle Adventures Nature Park & Zoo, a U.S. Highway 50 roadside attraction between Titusville and Orlando, has many large Alligators, Crocodiles, and other wild animals. A pontoon boat cruise on the jungle swamp gives visitors a look at the native wildlife. *Circa 1990s, $3-5.*

Nabbing a Crocodile. Owen Godwin, founder of Gatorland, poses for a picture with "Old Bonecrusher," a fourteen-foot, three-inch, 1,080-pound Crocodile. This large reptile was taken alive off Key Largo in a shark net in the mid-1950s. He was one of the world's largest captive Crocodiles when he died in 1970. *Circa 1950s, $3-5.*

An Alligator Show at Gatorama in Palmdale, Florida. *Circa 1950s, $3-5.*

Gatorland Walkway. A walkway near a lagoon full of lurking Alligators leads visitors into one of Florida's beautiful cypress swamps. The rustic walkway winds through tall stands of cypress trees and native plants. This Gatorland walkway allows visitors to get very close to many Alligators and exotic birds. *Circa 1990s, $2-4.*

Friendly neighbors? Alligators and birds live in a native ten-acre marsh and cypress swamp in the center of Gatorland. With one hundred females and twenty-five male gators, visitors are sure to catch a glimpse of Alligators in their natural habitat. One can also get a bird's-eye view from a three-story observation tower. Many native Florida birds and unique swamp critters also live in the native swamp. *Circa 1990s, $2-4.*

No Swimming! It's always wise to obey Alligator warning signs. This sign appears at the Jungle Adventures Nature Park & Zoo in Christmas. *Circa 1990s, $1-3.*

Feeding Goliath. The largest living Alligator at Jungle Adventures in Christmas is "Goliath;" he's fifteen feet long and is estimated to be seventy-seven years old. Here, he displays the jumping ability of Alligators. The green covering on the water is a water plant called duckweed. *Circa 1970s, $5-7.*

This is the last Card, I send you by mail,
The end of the Gator and the end of the "tale"

Huld's Puzzle Series No. 1-d.   Copyrighted 1905, by Franz Huld, Publisher, New York.

Crocodile Pit, Everglades Wonder Gardens, Bonita Springs, Florida.
Circa 1930s, $2-4.

Big Mo. "Big Mo," an 85-year old, 1,600-pound Alligator, is on exhibit at the Sanford Municipal Zoo. In addition to an upper and lower eyelid, the Alligator has a third transparent lid, to keep out the water when it dives. *Circa 1940s, $1-3.*

Real Photo Postcard. A real photo postcard of Alligators at the Everglades Wonder Gardens. An all-Florida exhibit with 2,000 Alligators, Crocodiles, snakes, animals, and birds teaches one about life in the mysterious Everglades. *Circa 1930s, $8-10.*

DC-88—The Parrot Jungle
Red Road, Miami, Fla.

PHOTO BY CHAS C. EBBETS

Beauty and the Beast. A pretty model looks at two large gators at the Parrot Jungle in Miami. This popular tourist attraction is a natural jungle of unspoiled tropical beauty. Photographers enjoy snapping pictures of macaws, parrots, cockatoos, pheasants, flamingos, and, of course, Alligators. *Cancelled 1940, $1-3.*

ALLIGATOR, PARROT JUNGLE, MIAMI, FLORIDA

An Alligator Mixes with Birds. At the Parrot Jungle in Miami, beautiful, rare birds fly free in a tropical paradise—brilliant Parrots and pink Flamingos—with quiet lakes and the intense color of tropical foliage and flowers. *Circa 1936, $1-3.*

600-pound Gator. This nearly 600-pound Alligator was photographed in captivity at Sarasota Jungle Gardens, a ten-acre tropical paradise located near downtown Sarasota. The gardens opened as a tourist attraction in 1940. Its creators have carved from a former banana plantation an enchanting garden complete with jungle paths and rare birds. *Circa 1945, $1-3.*

Homosassa Springs. A huge spring that flows at a rate of 70,000 gallons a minute is the chief source of water for the short Homosassa River, which empties into the Gulf of Mexico only nine miles to the west. Located north of Tampa, the springs are regarded as curious among naturalists because both fresh and salt-water fish seem equally at home in it. Homosassa Springs is known as nature's giant fish bowl. A few miles from the springs are the ruins of the great sugar plantation of Senator David Yulee, which was prosperous until Union soldiers destroyed it during the Civil War. *Circa 1950s, $1-3.*

Feeding time at Gator Lagoon. Daily Alligator feedings make an exciting spectacle for visitors to Homosassa Springs, where these fearsome reptiles live in a natural setting. More than fifty Alligators bask in the sun or thrash wildly about in the water in pursuit of bait. Feeding time is a photographer's delight as the large reptiles actually leap for their dinner. Alligators in captivity have learned to lunge out of the water like porpoises to catch tidbits of food. *Circa 1950s, $1-3.*

"Old Timer." An "Old Timer" in McKee Jungle Gardens just south of Vero Beach. These gardens include many rare plants, shrubs, and trees, robust towering palms, brightly blooming shrubs, a dense palm and oak forest, and overhanging live oak trees filled with orchids and air plants. *Cancelled 1948, $1-3.*

Ross Allen's Reptile Institute. One of Florida's most unusual attractions was Ross Allen's Reptile Institute. It housed one of the finest collections of live poisonous snakes, reptiles, and wild animals in the country. Tours included demonstrations and lectures in which the lecturer would enter various pens and cages with the animals, handle them, and discuss their habits, habitats, and other characteristics. A highlight of the tour was the demonstration-lecture staged in the poisonous snake pen. This view shows a large gator, "Old Cannibal," at the Reptile Institute. Ross Allen opened this attraction in 1940. *Cancelled 1952, $1-3.*

Big George. "Big George," a large Alligator at fourteen-feet, seven-inches, greeted visitors to Ross Allen's Reptile Institute at Silver Springs. *Circa 1940s, $1-3.*

Largest American Crocodile. Sobek, at the time believed to be the world's largest American Crocodile in the care of man, resided on Cypress Island at Silver Springs, near Ocala. The name "Sobek" refers to an Egyptian Crocodile god with the head of a Crocodile and the body of a man. *Circa 1970s, $2-4.*

88

Miracle Strip Jungle Land, West Panama City Beach

Alligator Pen. While the Weeki Wachee Springs, north of Clearwater, is chiefly noted for its mermaid shows, it offered an interesting wildlife display along the Weeki Wachee River. Part of this display was a pen of Alligators on the riverbank. Weeki Wachee is a natural spring, 137 feet deep, that forms the crystal-clear Weeki Wachee River, which rambles twelve miles through jungle country to the Gulf of Mexico. Here, these Alligators were part of gators on display at Weeki Wachee. *Circa 1950s, $1-3.*

Advertising Postcard. An advertising postcard of the Alligator Pool at Miracle Strip Jungle Land in Panama City Beach. This roadside attraction, which opened in 1965, was formerly the Ross Allen Jungle Show. Jungle Land was housed inside a towering artificial volcano. Live Animals were housed inside the volcano's base and one of the main attractions was the performing wildlife. Tour guides through Jungle Land were Sheena of the Jungle look-alikes wearing outfits as brief as standards of the day would permit. Most of the tour guides were supposed to be rainforest denizens or cave girls from the prehistoric past. *Circa 1960s, $3-5.*

Alligator Show.
A real photo postcard of an Alligator show at the "Sea Zoo" in South Daytona. Alligator shows such as this one teaches people about Alligators. The Sea Zoo attraction was founded as the Marine Life Laboratory in 1949 and was a popular stop for tourists. It expanded during the 1950s to include Alligator wrestling. *Circa 1955, $9-11.*

A new and thrilling sport at the Sea Zoo, Daytona Beach, Fla.

A New and Thrilling Sport.
A real photo postcard taken at the Sea Zoo in South Daytona, a small town south of Daytona Beach. An Alligator can seem quite docile, especially when someone is sitting on him. This popular roadside attraction gave its performing Alligators names like Methuselah and Narcissus. The Sea Zoo closed in 1970. *Circa 1960s, $9-11.*

TROPICAL PARK, DAYTONA BEACH, FLA.

COURTESY R. H. LE SESNE

7A-H2081

TAMPA ALLIGATOR FARM, SULPHUR SPRINGS PARK, FLORIDA.

Tropical Park. These saurians (Alligators and Crocodiles to most people) are basking in the warm sunshine in a native jungle beauty spot at Tropical Park in South Daytona. Some of these 'gators' did tricks for the entertainment of winter and summer visitors. The park, located on Ridgewood Avenue (U.S. Highway 1) at the intersection of Big Tree Road, was also, at one time, called the Daytona Beach Alligator Farm and included the original collection of "Alligator Joe" Campbell from Jacksonville. *Circa 1930s, $4-6.*

Tampa Alligator Farm. One of the boarders at the Tampa Alligator Farm in Sulphur Springs scoots down the slide and splashes into the Alligator pool. *Circa 1920s, $6-8.*

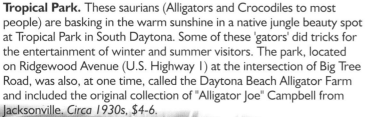

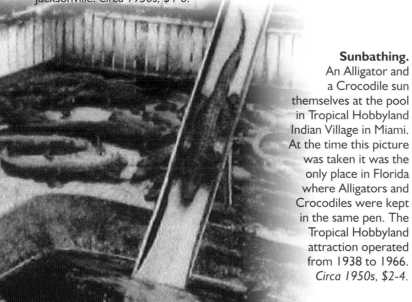

Hungry Alligators at Tropical Hobbyland, Miami, Florida

Sunbathing. An Alligator and a Crocodile sun themselves at the pool in Tropical Hobbyland Indian Village in Miami. At the time this picture was taken it was the only place in Florida where Alligators and Crocodiles were kept in the same pen. The Tropical Hobbyland attraction operated from 1938 to 1966. *Circa 1950s, $2-4.*

Florida Alligator Farm. This Florida Alligator Farm was located on U.S. Highway 1 north of Jacksonville. It included a free zoo with over 150 animals and reptiles. *Circa 1940s, $4-6.*

St. Petersburg Alligator Farm and Zoo. The St. Petersburg Alligator Farm and Zoo was founded in 1920 by Andrew Baker. The attraction, exhibited 1,500 Alligators, the largest weighing 1,200 pounds. A small zoo contained specimen of reptiles and Florida wild animals. The attraction operated until the mid-1940s. Animals from this farm were transferred to the Florida Wild Animal and Reptile Ranch in St. Petersburg. *Circa 1920s, $5-7.*

Baby Alligator and Eggs. In 1937, Dale Vaughn and F. W. Thomson opened the Florida Wild Animal and Reptile Ranch in St. Petersburg. Shown is a baby Alligator and eggs at the Ranch. *Circa 1930s, $2-4.*

Gator Feeding. Feeding an Alligator is one of the worst things people can do because it makes the gator associate food with humans. It's about as unwise as climbing a zoo fence to feed a cute tiger. Here, an Alligator is being fed at Gator Jungle. *Circa 1990s, $6-8.*

Gator Jungle. The Gator Jungle Alligator Farm was located on Interstate 4 between Plant City and Tampa. The business went belly up, and the gators disappeared, leaving a prime setting for other kinds of toothy critters. A family of Swedish carnival owners led by Christer Svensson bought the place and erected life-size dinosaur models among the existing ponds and paths. Dinosaur World became the world's largest dinosaur attraction. This twelve-acre outdoor museum is a subtropical jungle, with dinosaurs around virtually every corner. These remarkable fiberglass dinosaurs are made in Sweden. A 28-foot-high Brachiosarus replica and two forty-foot-high, fantasy-sized models of Tyrannosaurus Rex call attention to this roadside attraction along the Interstate highway. *Circa 1990s, $1-3.*

Alligator Farm, St. Andrew Bay, Fla.

Alligator Farm. An Alligator Pen at the Alligator Farm in St. Andrew Bay. *Circa 1920s, $8-10.*

Alligators in Tropical Florida. Alligators swim by sinuous movements of their muscular tail. On land, they are clumsy, slow, and deliberate, but can lunge quite fast if provoked. During the day, Alligators bask in the sun or rest with their bodies partially submerged. Even the crowds of people who flock to Florida's beaches do not enjoy sunbathing as much as these primeval cold-blooded reptiles. *Circa 1940s, $3-5.*

Alligators at Big Bear Park. *Circa 1930s, $2-4.*

Musa Isle Indian Village. The Musa Isle Indian Village in Miami was a Seminole Indian Trading Post, Alligator and Crocodile farm, museum, and a zoo. It was established in 1922 on the banks of the Miami River. The village was a place of tropical beauty and a popular attraction for tourists. Seminole Indian wrestlers entered a pool containing many Alligators and put on a thrilling and dangerous exhibition every hour from 9:30 a.m. to 6 p.m. In separate pools many more Alligators, from babies to several weighing over half a ton, were on display for visitors to see. Seminole Indian guides were on duty at all times. *Circa 1920s. $3-5.*

Souvenir of St. Augustine, Florida

I send you herewith the head of a Gator,
Watch for the mail – it will bring more later.

Teeth-brushing. An Alligator handler and Alligator perform for an audience at the St. Augustine Alligator Farm. *Circa 1920s, $10-12.*

Alligator Wrestling. At an Alligator show, the demonstrator drags, coaxes, and nudges the gators into performing for the audience. This includes wrestling matches with full-grown Alligators. Because Alligators have a brain half the size of a human thumbnail and are basically untamable, this can be a dangerous occupation. *Cancelled 1942, $2-4.*

Taking It Easy in Florida. An Alligator handler at the St. Augustine Alligator Farm takes a break from performing with the reptiles. *Circa 1930s, $3-5.*

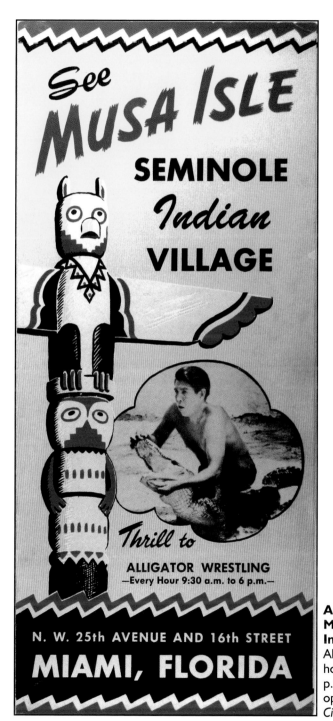

Real Photo Postcard. Alligators at the Musa Isle Indian Village in Miami. *Circa 1930s, $8-10*.

Advertising brochure, Musa Isle Seminole Indian Village, Miami. Alligator wrestling every hour from 9:30 a.m. to 6 p.m. This five-acre village opened in 1922. *Circa 1920s, $3-5*.

98

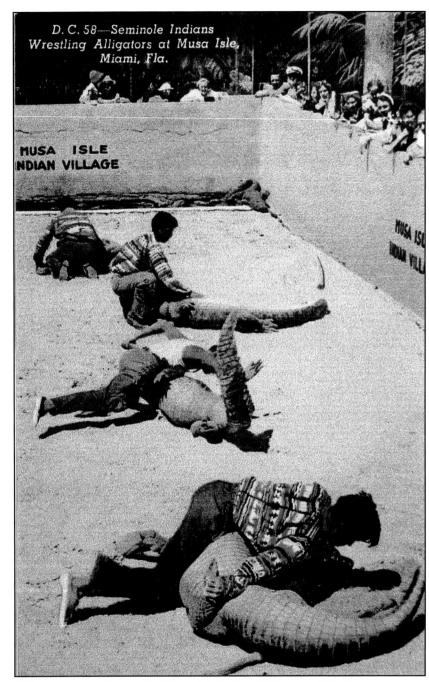

Alligator wrestling at the Musa Isle Indian Village in Miami.
Circa 1930s, $3-5.

Being Taught to Wrestle. Seminole youths are being taught to wrestle Alligators at the Musa Isle Seminole Indian Village. Since the early 1900s, there have been a number of places where men wrestle with live Alligators. Several of these were operated by Seminole Indians. *Circa 1930s, $3-5.*

MUSA ISLE SEMINOLE INDIAN VILLAGE

ALLIGATOR WRESTLING BY SEMINOLE INDIAN

Musa Isle Seminole Indian Village. Alligator wrestlers are unarmed and their only protection is a thorough knowledge of the animal's habits and anatomy. *Cancelled 1941, $2-4.*

MUSA ISLE SEMINOLE INDIAN VILLAGE

ALLIGATOR WRESTLING

Musa Isle Seminole Indian Village. Here, visitors could see unusual and thrilling exhibitions of handling and wrestling Alligators. The village also had a large collection of Crocodiles. *Circa 1930s, $3-5.*

Musa Isle Indian Village

Indian Boys Wrestling Alligator at Musa Isle

Indian Boys Wrestle Gator. A Seminole Indian boy wrestles an Alligator at the Musa Isle Indian Village on the Miami River. *Circa 1930s, $3-5.*

Open wide! Henry Nelson, a world champion Alligator wrestler, gave daily exhibitions of this ancient Seminole sport, at Tropical Hobbyland Indian Village in Miami. The pit at Tropical Hobbyland contained fifty Alligators and a dozen Crocodiles, yet Henry would go in the water with them entirely unarmed. *Circa 1940s, $3-5.*

Alligator Wrestling, Tropical Hobbyland, Miami, Florida

Performing Dangerous Stunts. One of the highlights of Alligator wrestling at Tropical Hobbyland Indian Village, 1525 N. W. 27th Avenue, Miami, is when Jackie Willis tucks the dangerous jaws under his chin and releases his hand hold. *Circa 1940s, $3-5.*

Alligator Wrestling. Another view of Henry Nelson performing with an Alligator at Tropical Hobbyland. *Circa 1940s, $3-5.*

Miccosukee Indian Wrestler. Shown is a Miccosukee Alligator wrestler at the Miccosukee Indian Village on the Tamiami Trail (U.S. Highway 41) west of Miami. *Circa 1950s, $1-3.*

Man versus Beast. A daredevil handler at Gatorland in Kissimmee grabbed this eight-foot Alligator by the tail and proceeded to conduct an "Old Florida" match of man versus beast. *Circa 2007, $2-4.*

Gator Wrestling. A Seminole Indian wrestles a gator at the Indian Zoo on the Old Dixie Highway in Fort Lauderdale. In addition to wrestling, visitors could see the Seminole Indians in their own surroundings. Many Seminoles made a living wrestling Alligators. *Circa 1950s, $3-5.*

Under Water Wrestling.
Gator wrestling underwater at the Ross Allen Reptile Institute at Silver Springs, the largest flowing springs in the world with over 750 million gallons daily. Temperature of the water is seventy-two degrees winter or summer. The wrestling exhibit was shown from sunrise to sunset, in all weather, every day of the year. *Circa 1940s, $4-6.*

WRESTLING ALLIGATOR UNDER WATER AT SILVER SPRINGS, FLA.

SA-H1371

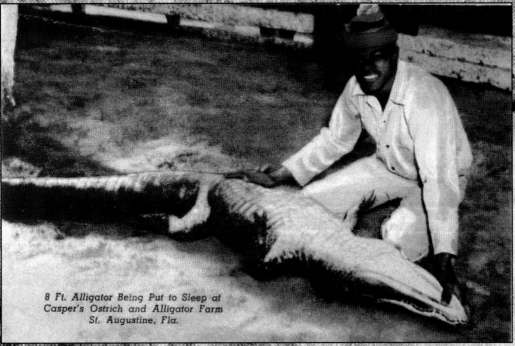

8 Ft. Alligator Being Put to Sleep at Casper's Ostrich and Alligator Farm St. Augustine, Fla.

Nap Time. Florida's famous Alligators have themselves become a tourist attraction. Though Alligator wrestling has always been a somewhat dubious pastime, it's a necessity for human survival in the swamplands. Here, a small gator is being put to sleep by a handler rubbing its stomach at Casper's Ostrich and Alligator Farm in St. Augustine. *Circa 1940s, $1-3.*

Two-thirds I am here, in body and soul,
The next is the last and the Gator is whole.

Florida Tourists.

Photo copyright 1907. The Hugh C. Leighton Co.

The Hugh G. Leighton Co. Alligators were a popular subject with publishers of Florida postcards. In the early 1900s, when picture postcards were at the height of their popularity, millions went through the postal system daily. Both photographers and artist-drawn Alligator scenes went on sale for locals and tourists to buy and send. Well-known comic artists used Alligators as the basis of postcard cartoons. *Cancelled 1910, $20-25.*

Marching through Florida. This postcard was published by Franz Huld in 1904 as part of his Alligator Postcard Series (*Huld's Alligator Series No. 1*). The sender of this comic card wrote, "This looks as though two is a company and three a crowd... I am just going downtown to mail my cards. Expect you will get a pile of them. The photographer has gone and I can't get my view cards now." *Cancelled 1908, $20-25.*

A Flying Trip through Florida

Driving through Florida. This comic postcard, produced by Franz Huld (*Huld's Alligator Series No. 6*), illustrates Alligator travel. *Cancelled 1906, $20-25.*

The Alligator Express. The sender of this postcard, mailed at DeLand on February 10, wrote, "I wish you were here. The weather is fine and you could play in the orange grove and eat all the oranges you could hold." *Cancelled 1914, $6-8.*

"Out for a Ride." Artists, photographers, cartoonists, and writers have been inspired by Florida's favorite reptile in the creation of paintings, cartoons, drawings, engravings, photographs, postcards, and stories that have entertained and enlightened the nation. The Alligator starred in Florida postcards in both real and fanciful ways. The Curt Teich Co. in Chicago published this postcard. *Circa 1920s, $6-8.*

Alligator race. *Circa 1913, $6-8.*

GREETINGS FROM FLORIDA.

134 HITTING ON ALL FOUR, THE ALLIGATOR IN THE SUNSHINE STATE. FLORIDA

The Gator in the Sunshine State. The sender of this postcard wrote, "This is the way the girls spend their time in Florida." *Cancelled 1930, $2-4.*

10157 — *Florida Playmates.*

Greetings from Florida. *Circa 1910s, $8-10.*

Florida Playmates. A little girl playing with two stuffed Alligators. The card was published by M. Mark in Jacksonville and printed in Germany. *Circa 1908, $4-6.*

878 ALL DRESSED UP TO MEET YOU IN FLORIDA

All Dressed Up to Meet You in Florida.
An Alligator may never win a beauty contest, but they rank high in
popularity with visitors to Florida. *Cancelled 1937, $4-6.*

Feeding the Alligator.
The sender of this card, mailed in Jacksonville, wrote, "How would you like a pet of this kind?"
Of course, he didn't admit that this was a stuffed Alligator. *Cancelled 1914, $5-7.*

"I Love A Fat Man!"
The sender of this postcard by H. Horina wrote,
"They also like dogs." Want to attract an Alligator?
Bring your dog with you to a river or lake. Dogs
are usually low to the ground and often resemble
other animals that are the Alligator's natural prey:
raccoons and otters. Dogs also tend to be noisy
and splash around, which excites Alligators.
Cancelled 1912, $10-12.

"Ain't This a Cruel World?" An H. Horina comic postcard.
Cancelled 1911, $10-12.

"Won't You Be My Honey?"
Cancelled 1911, $10-12.

Comic postcard by H. Horina. *Circa 1911, $10-12.*

**Comic postcard
by H. Horina.**
How could anyone call
these Alligators ugly!
Circa 1911, $10-12.

110

The Alligator Circus. Copyrighted by Havens in 1893.
Cancelled 1912, $5-7.

Gators Singing. Printed on this postcard, postmarked in Daytona Beach, is the message, "The Alligator Quartette Singing Way Down Upon The Suwannee River." *Cancelled 1912, $6-8.*

A Florida Alligator Chorus. Cancelled 1913, $9-11.

The Private Lesson. This postcard, part of the Florida Artistic Series, was published by the H. & W. B. Drew Co. in Jacksonville. Photograph was copyrighted by Havens in 1893. *Circa 1910, $9-11.*

Singing Alligators. *Circa 1920s, $5-7.*

Huld's Alligator Series No. 4. Copyrighted 1904 by Franz Huld, Publisher, New York.

Floating in Florida. This humorous postcard was published by Franz Huld in 1904 as part of his Alligator Postcard Series *(Huld's Alligator Series No. 4). Cancelled 1907, $5-7.*

Homeward Bound, Florida

Homeward Bound, you're right we are
As fast as a ninety horsepower car.
This is our twelve-foot motorboat
Safe as long as it keeps afloat."

--L. M. Thornton

A Gator Poem. *Cancelled 1928, $4-6.*

14. HOMEWARD BOUND, FLORIDA.

Homeward Bound, you're right we are,
As fast as a ninety horsepower car,
This is our twelve foot motor boat
Safe as long as it keeps afloat.
—L. M. THORNTON.

21401

Greetings from Florida. Accept a box of kumquats and the baby Alligators, with my best wishes and greetings from Florida. The sender of this card wrote, "Received your letter, but I am to lazy to write a letter." *Cancelled 1913, $5-7.*

Accept my Best Wishes and Compliments from the Sunny South. *Circa 1913, $5-7.*

Alligator Bait in Florida. As depicted in the next several images, African Americans were the butt of humor and satire in many early 1900s postcards. Exaggerated situations on postcard images, not unusual for the time in racial attitude, now provide insight into the white Floridian conception of African American life and livelihood. *Cancelled 1911, $8-10.*

114

"Honey Come Down"—I Am Waiting for You in Florida. *Circa 1920s, $5-7.*

Musa Isle Indian Village. The Musa Isle Indian Village in Miami published this postcard view. *Circa 1920s, $8-10.*

A Joy Ride in Florida. *Circa 1920s, $5-7.*

In a Tight Place.

In a Tight Place. Max Mark, a Jacksonville photographer who published several postcards around Jacksonville and St. Augustine, also did this Alligator card. It shows a small sub-adult Alligator lurching out of tropical fauna to bite a terrified man. The action was, of course, staged. It was common practice to use stuffed Alligators for such photographs, and Mark undoubtedly followed suit. *Circa 1906, $8-10.*

DON'T KNOW WHETHER I'M GOING OR COMING BUT I'M ON MY WAY

Don't be afraid of dropping in— you are welcome.

Don't be Afraid of Dropping In—You Are Welcome. *Cancelled 1919, $5-7.*

"Don't know whether I'm going or coming, but I'm on my way." A Bamforth Comic Postcard. *Circa 1926, $4-6.*

Alligator Humor.
"There is a fine opening here for you."
I wonder if that has a bottom to it.
Cancelled 1909, $5-7.

A Novelty Alligator Postcard.
The moving eye of this card is enclosed in a clear
plastic bubble. *Circa 1940s, $4-6.*

At Famous Florida's Silver Springs

At Famous Florida's Silver Springs.
"Signs that read NO SWIMMING ALLOWED should be obeyed..."
says this lovely violator, after being dramatically rescued from a giant
Crocodile by Ross Allen at his Reptile Institute at Florida's Silver
Springs. This was a staged postcard scene. *Cancelled 1934, $3-5.*

Comic Alligator Postcard.
The sender of this card wrote, "Enjoying our stay
here at Jensen Beach. Visited Miami today. Saw
Jackie Gleason's eating place. He features 'How
sweet it is' ham sandwich for 65 cents."
Cancelled 1971, $2-4.

Dancing Gator. This illustration by Heinrich Kley is a very strange drawing of an Alligator. The lady seems to be perfectly calm about a double hazard—falling on the ice and her odd skating companion. *Circa 1930s, $3-5.*

This is the last Card I send you by mail,
The end of the Gator and the end of the "tale."

Samuel Langsdorf & Company of New York published a variety of postcards including a Shell Border Series, a thirty-card series of State/Beautiful Women postcards, and the popular Alligator Border Series postcards. These cards were designed in the United States and sent to Germany for printing. This resulted in exceptional color quality.

Each Alligator Border postcard featured the same trio of smiling Alligators surrounding a different image. An embossing process that raised them above the rest of the card further accented the Alligators. There are 165 postcards in the Alligator Border Series. These postcards are in much demand by present-day collectors. They are about one hundred years old and feature scenes from Florida at the beginning of the twentieth century. A complete set of Alligator Border postcards is valued at somewhere around $9,000 to $11,000. Individual cards are often priced in the range of $30-$100.

The following list indicates popular Florida cities and topics of the period:

- Nine cards of Miami (Card numbers 500-507, 532)
- Fourteen cards of Key West (Card numbers 508-517, 661-664)
- Fifteen cards of Palm Beach (Card numbers 518-531, 533)
- Ten cards of Palatka (Card numbers 534-543)
- Sixteen cards of St. Augustine (Card numbers 544-559)
- Twenty-three cards of Tampa (Card numbers 560-582)
- Twenty-four cards of Jacksonville (Card numbers 583-606)
- Ten cards of Ormond (Card numbers 607-616)
- Nine cards of Daytona (Card numbers 617-620, 622-626)
- One card of Fort Pierce (Card number 621)
- Eleven cards of agriculture related scenes (Card numbers 627-637)
- Twenty-three miscellaneous card scenes (Card numbers 638-660)

Alligators, Natives of Florida, S596. The Alligator Border Series was published by Langsdorf. The design is unique and the quality of printing excellent. Many collectors save these cards and their prices are steadily increasing. This view illustrates Alligators on display at an Alligator farm. *Cancelled 1919, $30-100.*

Light House, Key West, Florida, S617. Hurricanes devastated Key West many times during the twentieth century, but the lighthouse endured them all. In 1915 the lighthouse was automated. Ernest Hemingway lived in a house across the street from the lighthouse. Today, the lighthouse is a popular tourist attraction. *Circa 1908, $30-100.*

Greetings from the Sunny South, The Latest Thing Out, S660. These baby Ostriches, new arrivals at this Ostrich Farm in Jacksonville, would grow to be large birds that could run at speeds of forty miles per hour. *Circa 1908, $30-100.*

Canoeing on the Upper Tomoka, near Ormond, S616. Canoeing is an excellent way to view the scenic beauty and wildlife on the Tomoka River near Ormond Beach. This Alligator Border view shows a canoeist enjoying the water. *Circa 1908, $30-100.*

Rapid transit at Fort Pierce, Indian River, Florida, S621. This Alligator Border postcard shows an oxen-pulled wagon hauling crates of oranges from a citrus grove to the Fort Pierce Steamboat dock on the Indian River. *Circa 1908, $30-100.*

Picking Oranges, Florida, S629. Ella Mae mailed this Alligator Border postcard showing workers picking oranges in Florida. The citrus industry is big business in Florida, and it all begins with the workers who pick the fruit from the tree—one orange at a time. This hard work is the start of a long process that brings ripe oranges to the consumer. *Cancelled 1908, $30-100.*

Grape Fruit Grove, Florida, S628.
The grapefruit is one of Florida's gifts to the world. The pink and seedless grapefruit were both developed in Florida. This Alligator Border view shows a grove of trees loaded with grapefruit. *Circa 1908, $30-100.*

Ruins of the old Sugar Mill, Bulow Plantation, near Ormond, S607. This Alligator Border postcard shows the stone wall ruins of the Bulow Plantation, which was destroyed by Seminole Indians in 1836. *Circa 1908, $30-100.*

Old Sugar House built in 1705, Port Orange, near Daytona, S617. This Alligator Border view, postmarked at Holly Hill, illustrates an old English Sugar Mill built in Port Orange. The ruins have been restored in a lovely garden setting, with thousands of flowering plants, live oak trees, and sweeping lawns. Sugar-making equipment has been refined, but the present day method is not unlike that of more than a century ago. *Cancelled 1908, $30-100.*

A Residence Embowered in Cocoanut Trees, Key West, S663. This Alligator Border postcard shows a Key West residence surrounded by subtropical plants, including cocoanut trees. *Circa 1908, $30-100.*

124

Tampa Bay Hotel, Tampa, S571. This Alligator Border view illustrates Henry Plant's unique Tampa Bay Hotel. The magnificent hotel opened with a grand ball February 5, 1891. It's the most distinctive landmark in Tampa. Horseshoe arches and Byzantine silver domes combine with Moorish minarets to give the hotel a look like none other. *Circa 1908, $30-100.*

Hotel Ponce de Leon, St. Augustine, S658. In 1888, Henry M. Flagler built a resort hotel in St. Augustine that rivaled the best hotels in the world. Many important visitors climbed the steps of the Ponce including five United States presidents. *Circa 1908, $30-100.*

County Court House, Key West, S514.
The first Monroe County courthouse was constructed originally as a military barracks, was later used as a hospital, and eventually remodeled to serve as the courthouse. This Alligator Border postcard illustrates the new brick Key West County Courthouse that was built in 1890. *Cancelled 1914, $30-100.*

Magnolia Street, Daytona, S623. A Magnolia Street scene in downtown Daytona (now Daytona Beach) is illustrated on this Alligator Border postcard. *Cancelled 1908, $30-100.*

Ridgewood Avenue and Ridgewood Hotel, Daytona, S619. This Alligator Border view shows Ridgewood Avenue (U.S. Highway 1) and the Ridgewood Hotel in downtown Daytona (now Daytona Beach). This tree-lined road connected Daytona with New Smyrna in the south and Ormond in the North. *Circa 1908, $30-100.*

Tropical Street Scene, Key West, S615. This vertical Alligator Border postcard view is of cocoanut palm trees and other subtropical plants in Key West, the southernmost city in the United States. *Circa 1908, $30-100.*

Ormond Hotel, Ormond, S610.
The Ormond Hotel opened in 1888 in Ormond (now Ormond Beach), a community just north of Daytona Beach. In 1890, Henry M. Flagler bought the hotel and made it one of the most popular winter resorts in Florida. *Circa 1908, $30-100.*

Bethosoda Church, Palm Beach, Florida, S528.
This Alligator Border postcard, addressed to Earl Piper in Hillside, Pennsylvania, was cancelled eight times. *Cancelled 1911, $30-100.*

12th Street Looking East, Miami, Florida, S602. *Circa 1908, $30-100.*

Franklin Street, Tampa, S580. Tampa's first form of public transportation was provided by the Tampa Street Railway Company in 1886. By 1913 Tampa had a unified streetcar system throughout the city. This view of Franklin Street shows a glimpse of the Hillsborough County Courthouse. *Circa 1908, $30-100.*

Lemon Street, Palatka, S535. By 1870 Palatka was a thriving village with several stores, two churches, and two steam mills. Two large hotels (the Putnam House and St. Johns House) had opened to accommodate tourists. This Alligator Border view shows Lemon Street (now St. Johns Avenue) in downtown Palatka. *Circa 1908, $30-100.*

The Royal Palm and Miami River, Florida, S601. Henry M. Flagler's famous Royal Palm Hotel, finished in 1897, made Miami an important tourist resort. The five-story, 350-room Royal Palm, surrounded by citrus groves and gardens, looked out on the beautiful blue waters of Biscayne Bay and the Miami River. The structure was torn down in 1930. *Circa 1908, $30-100.*

Steamer *Fred de Bary* on St. Johns River, Florida, S543. A trip by Steamboat along the wild and weird St. Johns River was one of the greatest attractions for all Florida tourists in the 1800s and early 1900s. Gliding along the river, visitors saw on the banks large orange groves, flourishing little communities, exotic sub-tropical vegetation, and interesting wildlife, including Alligators. A panorama completely different to Northern visitors, but one remembered vividly long after the boat trip was over. This Alligator Border view shows the *Frederick DeBary* Steamboat, an iron-hulled, side-wheeler vessel that was 145.5 feet long and 24.2 feet wide. The *Frederick DeBary* ran daily from Jacksonville to Enterprise on Lake Monroe. Among her famous passengers was President Chester Arthur. *Circa 1908, $30-100.*

The *Crescent* on St. Johns River, Palatka, S540. The 84-gross ton, steel-hull, 120-foot long *Crescent* Steamboat was built in 1893 in Jacksonville. This Alligator Border view shows the *Crescent* sailing on St. Johns River. *Circa 1908, $30-100.*

On the Ocklawaha River, Florida, S541. The *Astatula* Steamboat traveling on the picturesque Ocklawaha River is illustrated on this Alligator Border postcard. The Ocklawaha flows over sixty miles in a northern direction to St. Johns River. Its primary tributary is the Silver River, the outflow from Silver Springs. One passenger from 1902 wrote, "The visitor to Florida who misses a trip up the Ocklawaha River on one of the famous river Steamboats of the Hart Line fails to behold the greatest attraction of the state." *Circa 1908, $30-100*

At the Wharf, Palatka, S534. Steamboat passengers on St. Johns River often stopped in Palatka for an overnight stay or to transfer to another Steamboat going to Silver Springs or Crescent City on Crescent Lake. Palatka was a St. Johns River city located midway between Jacksonville and Sanford. In the 1880s, twenty-five or thirty Steamboats could usually be counted at the wharf every day and tourists sometimes had to beg for accommodations in a town of nine hotels and five hundred rooms. *Circa 1908, $30-100.*

Left: *S. S. Miami*, **S508.**
This Alligator Border view is of the *S. S. Miami* Steamship, which was part of Henry M. Flagler's fleet that sailed between Miami and Havana, Cuba. *Circa 1908, $30-100.*

Greetings from the Sunny South: A Watermelon Feast, S644.
Circa 1908, $30-100.

Greetings from the Sunny South: At Leisure, S639. This view shows two dock workers taking a break (probably at the Jacksonville or Palatka Steamboat docks). *Circa 1908, $30-100.*

This *Greetings from the Sunny South* series is meant to show early African American life in Florida during a time when racism was rampant. African Americans were often the butt of humor and satire in many early 1900s postcards, and these images were included for historical purposes only.

Greetings from the Sunny South: The Smile that won't come off, S638. *Circa 1910, $30-100.*

Greetings from the Sunny South: A Cotton Picker, S640. This field worker is illustrating the basket that she uses when picking cotton. *Circa 1908, $30-100.*

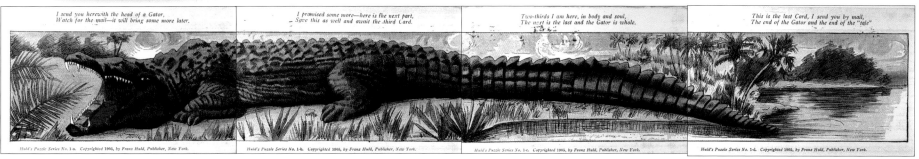

I send you herewith the head of a Gator,
Watch for the mail---it will bring some more later.

I promised some more--here is the next part,
Save this as well and await the third Card.

Two-thirds I am here, in body and soul,
The next is the last and the Gator is whole.

This is the last Card, I send you by mail,
The end of the Gator and the end of the "tail."

Circa 1905

I send you herewith the head of a Gator,
Watch for the mail---it will bring more later.

Two-thirds I am here, in body and soul,
The next is the last and the Gator is whole.

This is the last Card, I send you by mail,
The end of the Gator and the end of the "tail."

Circa 2002

First Came the Head ... Installment cards were popular novelty items in the early 1900s. The sender would purchase sets of cards that, when placed in sequence, formed a unified scene. The cards were mailed in consecutive order over a period of time. This set of four Alligator cards was produced by Franz Huld, Publisher, *copyrighted 1905. (Huld's Puzzle Series No. 1-a, 1-b, 1-c, 1-d). Cancelled 1908, $45-50.*

A three-card Alligator souvenir of St. Augustine, Florida. *Circa 2002, $8-10.*

Brochure.
General information brochure introduces readers to Florida's favorite reptile—the Alligator. The brochure was produced by several organizations including Gatorland, Billie Swamp Safari, *Florida Living Magazine,* and the Florida Alligator Marketing & Education Advisory Committee.
Circa 2005, Free.

All the Way from Florida

321

An Exaggerated Alligator Postcard. This card was one of thousands of larger-than-life postcards that photographers produced early in the 1900s. If local animals could be photographed, they figured, they were fair game for exaggeration through technical trickery.
Circa 1930s, $4-6.

Big Cement Gators.
At one time, there was an unofficial contest to see which Florida tourist attraction could build the biggest cement Alligator. The results are all over the state. There's a 124-foot gator with a Land Rover in its jaws at Kissimmee's defunct Jungleland Zoo. Up the road, near Orlando, is the famous entrance to Gatorland through the toothy creature's open mouth. The biggest concrete gator, 220 feet from snout to tail tip, is Swampy at Jungle Adventures between Orlando and Titusville.
Circa 1990s, $3-5.

"The Home Stretch In Florida." Published by the Curt Teich Company, Chicago. *Circa 1910, $5-7.*

I Came to Florida to See the Sights—and Now I Am One of Them. *Circa 1940s, $2-4.*

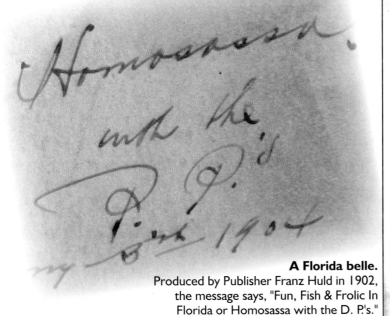

A Florida belle. Produced by Publisher Franz Huld in 1902, the message says, "Fun, Fish & Frolic In Florida or Homosassa with the D. P.'s." *Cancelled 1904, $5-7.*

A Florida Belle.

No. 262. Copyright, 1902, by Franz Huld, Publisher, New York

134

Hunter or Bait? Early visitors to Florida were fascinated with Alligators. Views with the Alligator motif were popular with the tourist. Most photographers included a stuffed Alligator in their props. Tourists and residents alike loved to have their pictures taken with the fierce-looking reptile. Here, a Miami tourist poses for a photograph. *Circa 1910, $8-10.*

Florida Tourists Pose for Photo Postcard with Stuffed Alligators.
Circa 1930s, $8-10.

Tourist Poses for Photo Postcard in Miami. *Circa 1930, $8-10.*

Miami Tourist Poses for Photo Postcard. *Circa 1920s, $8-10.*

Private Mailing Card from a Cape Coral Dentist. *Circa 1980, $2-4.*

Feeding the Alligators in Florida. A happy little visitor to one of the Sunshine State's great Alligator farms where Alligators were raised for their much-prized skin. These tiny fellows were often kept as pets prior to 1960. *Circa 1930s, $3-5.*

Close-up of a Fourteen-Foot Crocodile Head. *Circa 1940s, $1-3.*

Send More Tourists—the Last Ones were Delicious! *Circa 2006, $1-3.*

The Eye of the Gator. As Alligators hunt at night, their eyes have the typical vertical slit-like pupil. The advantage of this is that it permits more light to enter the eye and register on the retina than would be possible with a round pupil. The eyes of the Alligator appear to glow in the dark when light is shined at them. With a mixture of both rods and cones forming the retina, Alligators possess color vision. When hunting underwater, the eyes are protected by the transparent nictitating membranes, but clear vision may be difficult in muddy water. *Circa 2007, $1-3.*

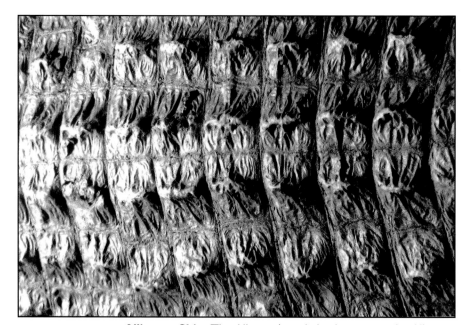

Alligator Skin. The Alligator's scaly back protects the Alligator from enemies and also from the sun. The armor is often able to withstand the impact of knives or spears. *Circa 2007, $1-3.*

Gator teeth. The teeth of Alligators are potentially lethal and the force of the jaws when they close will drive the teeth well into their victim's flesh. The teeth, conical in shape with sharp points, are anchored in their sockets by connective tissue. The teeth are constantly growing and being shed throughout the Alligator's life. In very old gators, however, lost teeth may not be replaced. An Alligator's teeth are well suited for inflicting maximum injury on prey and retaining a firm grip. If the prey is too large to swallow in one gulp, they tear it apart. Sometimes they drag large prey below the surface, where it drowns. *Circa 2007, $1-3.*

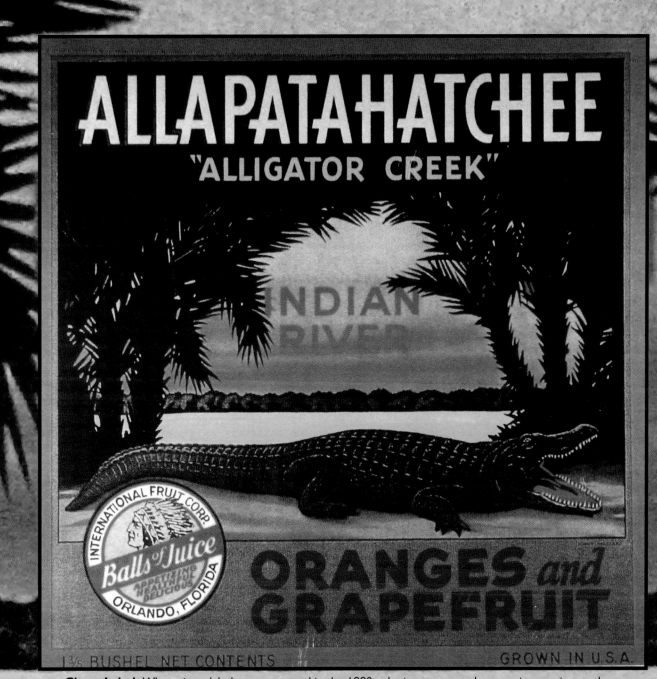

ALLAPATAHATCHEE

"ALLIGATOR CREEK"

INDIAN
RIVER

INTERNATIONAL FRUIT CORP.
Balls of Juice
APPETIZING
HEALTHFUL
DELICIOUS
ORLANDO, FLORIDA

ORANGES *and* GRAPEFRUIT

1⅗ BUSHEL NET CONTENTS   GROWN IN U.S.A.

Citrus Label. When citrus labels were created in the 1880s, the intent was to leave an impression so the citrus buyer would remember to order that particular brand of fruit. The colorful fruit label was pasted on the ends of the wooden fruit crates. This citrus label depicting an Alligator was used to inform buyers that the oranges and grapefruit came from the International Fruit Corp. in Orlando. *Circa 1930s, $100-110.*

The Gator Diner at Central Avenue and 20th Street, St. Petersburg. Many other restaurants and businesses use the Alligator theme in their business names: Alligator Pool Service, Gator Pools, Gator Towing, Alligator Graphics, Gator Office Supply, Gator Investments, Alligator Leasing, Gator Freightways, Gator Club, Gator Shoe Corporation, Gator Carwash, Gator Plumbing, Gator Boats, Alligator Bar, and Gator Plastics. There is no apparent end to the ever-increasing use of the Alligator in business names, trademarks, logos, and products. *Circa 1951, $10-12.*

The Mascot. The University of Florida, the state's oldest and largest university, was established in Gainesville in 1853. The university campus size is about 2,000 acres and has a student enrolment of over 44,000. In 1908 UF got a new mascot—the "Alligator," which later was condensed to "Gator." Albert and Alberta, students in gator costumes, help students cheer the UF Gator football and basketball teams to victory. The UF student newspaper is called *The Alligator.* Shown is the UF football stadium, called "the Swamp," and covers of old UF football programs. *Circa 2007, $3-5.*

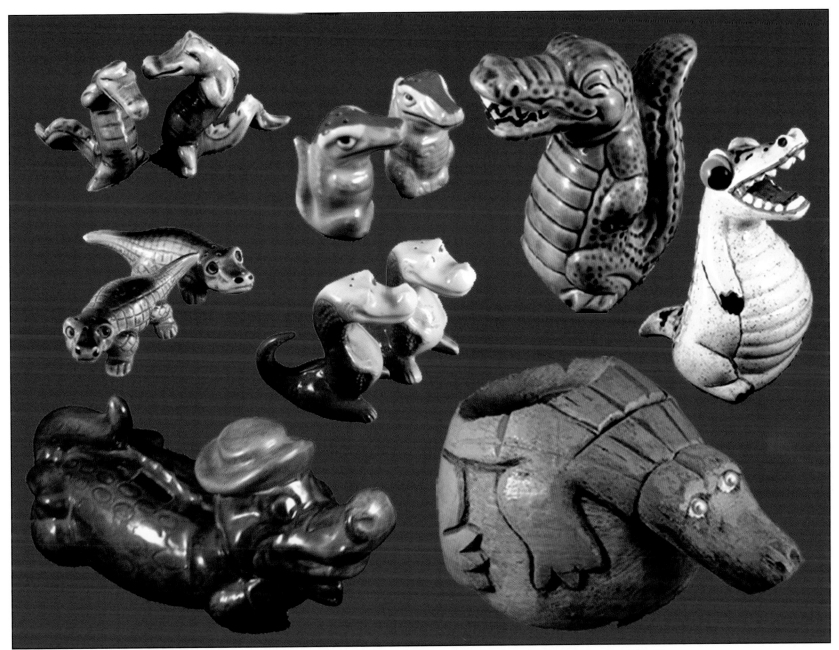

Alligator Souvenirs. Salt shakers, top left corner, *$12-14;* ceramic figurines, top right corner, *$20-22;* bank, bottom left corner, *$22-24;* and cocoanut cup or planter, bottom right corner, *$14-16.*

A Cute Alligator Figurine. *Circa 1980s, $8-10.*

Bibliography

Some of the titles in this list are currently in print and are available in bookstores. Other books in this list are out of print, however, they may be available in your local public library or from a used bookstore.

Adams, William R. and Carl Shiver. *The St. Augustine Alligator Farm: A Complete History*. St. Augustine, Florida: Southern Heritage Press, 2005.

Adams, William R. *The Legend of Gomek*. St. Augustine, Florida: St. Augustine Alligator Farm, 1999.

Alderton, David. *Crocodiles & Alligators of the World*. New York: Facts on File, Inc., 1991.

Behler, John and Deborah Behler. *Alligators & Crocodiles*. Stillwater, Minnesota: Voyageur Press, Inc., 1998.

Blassingame, Wyatt. *Wonders of Alligators and Crocodiles*. New York, New York: Dodd, Mead & Company, 1973.

Bothwell, Dick. *The Great Outdoors Book of Alligators*. St. Petersburg, Florida: Great Outdoors Publishing Co., 1962.

Dow, Leslie. *Alligators and Crocodiles*. New York, New York: Facts on File, 1990.

Fairweather, Gari D. *Alligators and Other Crocodilians*. Chicago, Illinois: World Book, Inc., 2003.

Fitzgerald, Patrick J. *Croc and Gator Attacks*. New York, New York: Children's Press, 2000.

Garlock, Michael. *Killer Gators and Crocs*. Guilford, Connecticut. Lyons Press, 2006.

Gatorland Zoo. Kissimmee, Florida: Godwin's Gatorland, Inc., 1979.

Glasgow, Vaughn L. *A Social History of the American Alligator*. New York, New York: St. Martin's Press, 1991.

Guggisberg, C. A. W. *Crocodiles: Their natural history, folklore and conservation*. Harrisburg, Pennsylvania: Stackpole Books, 1972.

Hartley, William and Ellen Hartley. *The Alligator: King of the Wilderness*. Nashville, Tennessee: Thomas Nelson, Inc., Publishers, 1977.

Jenkins, Edward G. *Guide to Florida*. New York, New York: American News Company, 1875.

Lauber, Patricia. *Alligators: A Success Story*. New York, New York: Henry Holt and Company, 1993.

Levy, Charles. *Crocodiles & Alligators*. London, England: Eagle Editions Ltd., 2003.

Lockwood, C. C. *The Alligator Book*. Baton Rouge, Louisiana: Louisiana State University Press, 2002.

Lockwood Sophie. *Crocodiles*. Charleston, Minnesota: The Child's World, 2006.

Mahoney, Lawrence T. *Gator: An Eye-Opening Adventure*. Berkeley, California: Ten Speed Press, 1991.

Markle, Sandra. *Outside and Inside Alligators*. New York, New York: Atheneum Books, 1998.

McCarthy, Kevin M. *Alligator Tales*. Sarasota, Florida: Pineapple Press, Inc., 1998.

St. Johns River Guidebook. Sarasota, Florida: Pineapple Press, 2004.

Packard, Winthrop. *Florida Trails*. Boston, Massachusetts: Small, Maynard and Company, 1910.

Patent, Dorothy Hinshaw. *The American Alligator*. New York, New York: Clarion Books, 1994.

Perrero, Laurie. *Alligators and Crocodiles of the World*. Miami, Florida: Winward Publishing, Inc., 1975.

Ricciuti, Edward R. *The American Alligator: Its Life in the Wild*. New York, New York: Harper & Row, Publishers, 1972.

Ross, Charles A., Editor. *Crocodiles and Alligators*. New York, New York: Facts on File, 1989.

Shaffer, Michael and Andrew Fleming. *Bathroom Book of Florida Trivia: Weird, Wacky and Wild*. Blue Bike Books, 2007.

Shaw, Evelyn. *Alligator*. New York, New York: Harper & Row, Publishers, 1972.

Simon, Seymour. *Crocodiles & Alligators*. New York, New York: Harper Collins, Publishers, 1999.

Sleeper, Barbara. *Beneath the Blackwater Alligators*. Minocqua, Wisconsin: Northword Press, Inc., 1996.

Snyder, Trish. *Alligator & Crocodile Rescue*. Buffalo, New York: Firefly Books, 2006.

Sobczyak, Charles. *Alligators, Sharks & Panthers: Deadly Encounters with Florida's Top Predator—Man*. Sanibel, Florida: Indigo Press, 2007.

Stone, Lynn M. *Alligators and Crocodiles*. Chicago, Illinois: Children's Press, 1989.

Stoops, Erik D. and Debbie Lynne Stone. *Alligators & Crocodiles*. New York, New York: Sterling Publishing Company, 1994.

Strawn, Martha A. *Alligators: Prehistoric Presence in the American Landscape*. Baltimore, Maryland: John Hopkins University Press, 1997.

Van Meter, Victoria Brook. *Florida's Alligators and Crocodiles*. Miami, Florida: Florida Power and Light, 1987.

Wexo, John Bonnett. *Alligators & Crocodiles*. Poway, California: Wildlife Education, Ltd., 2003.

Winterbotham Ann L. and George R. Campbell. *About Alligators*. Fort Myers, Florida: Sutherland Publishing, 1985.

Zim, Herbert S. *Alligators and Crocodiles*. New York, New York: William Morrow & Company, 1952.

Index